PUSHKIN
THE BRONZE HORSEMAN

Statue of Peter the Great. Engraved for the London Encyclopaedia 1823.

А.С. ПУШКИН
МЕДНЫЙ ВСАДНИК

A.S. PUSHKIN
THE BRONZE HORSEMAN

EDITED WITH INTRODUCTION, NOTES,
BIBLIOGRAPHY & VOCABULARY
BY MICHAEL BASKER

RUSSIAN
STUDIES

PUBLISHED BY BRISTOL CLASSICAL PRESS
GENERAL EDITOR: JOHN H. BETTS
RUSSIAN TEXTS SERIES EDITOR: NEIL CORNWELL

This impression 2003
This edition published in 2000 by
Bristol Classical Press
an imprint of
Gerald Duckworth & Co. Ltd.
61 Frith Street, London W1D 3JL
Tel: 020 7434 4242
Fax: 020 7434 4420
inquiries@duckworth-publishers.co.uk
www.ducknet.co.uk

A catalogue record for this book is available
from the British Library

ISBN 1 85399 575 4

CONTENTS

BIOGRAPHICAL NOTES

Aleksandr Sergeevich Pushkin (1799-1837)

1799   Born 26 May. Father of old aristocratic lineage; mother the granddaughter of General A. Gannibal (the 'Negro of Peter the Great').

1811-17   Educated at newly opened Imperial Lycée at Tsarskoe Selo. First poetry.

1817-20   Nominal appointment in Foreign Office, St Petersburg. Life of dissipation. 'Free-thinking' acquaintances (future Decembrists).

1820   Completes first major narrative poem, *Ruslan and Liudmila (Руслáн и Людмúла)*. Exiled to south for handful of 'liberal' verses on freedom and serfdom.

1820-4   Southern exile (Ekaterinoslav/Kishinev/Odessa). 'Byronic' period; narrative poems include *The Captive of the Caucasus (Кавкáзский плéнник,* 1820-1), *The Fountain of Bakhchisarai (Бахчисарáйский фонтáн,* 1822). Begins novel in verse *Evgenii Onegin* (1823). Recognition as leading poet of generation.

1824-6   Exile continues at parental estate of Mikhailovskoe. *The Gypsies (Цыгáны,* 1824); *Count Nulin (Граф Нýлин), Boris Godunov* (1825). 'Misses' flood of 1824, and Decembrist Revolt of 1825.

1826   Sept.: summoned to Moscow by Nicholas I. Freed from exile, with tsar as personal censor; subject to 'surveillance, guidance and counselling' of Count Benkendorf, Head of the Third Section (Secret Police). Return to dissolute way of life; but search for stability.

1828   *Poltava.*

1829   4-month visit to Transcaucasia.

1830   Proposes to Natal'ia Goncharova. Sept.-Nov: stranded by cholera epidemic at new estate; his first 'Boldino autumn': *Onegin*; lyrics; *Little Tragedies*; *Tales of Belkin (Пóвести Бéлкина)*; *Little House at Kolomna (Дóмик в Колóмне)*.

1831   Marries in Feb. Settles in Petersburg. Completes *Onegin*.

1833   Historical research. Travels to Urals. Second Boldino autumn (see Introduction).

1833-5   *The Captain's Daughter (Капитáнская дóчка).*

1833-6   Unhappy period in St Petersburg; humiliations at court, debts, marital insecurity. Little creative work.

1837   Goaded into duel with D'Anthès, adopted son of Dutch ambassador, on 27 January. Shot in stomach. Died two days later. 'Secret' burial decreed, to avoid expressions of public sympathy.

INTRODUCTION

The Bronze Horseman, Pushkin's last and best narrative poem, was written at Boldino in autumn 1833. It dates from a difficult period in Pushkin's life, during which he felt himself chronically frustrated by the social and financial circumstances of domestic life in St Petersburg, and unable to devote himself fully to his creative work. In mid-August 1833, he therefore contrived a short break from the Russian capital. He had obtained the permission of Tsar Nicholas I to travel to the Urals, where it was his undeclared intention to seek eyewitness accounts which would supplement and conclude his research into the Pugachev Rebellion of 1773-5. From Kazan', Orenburg and Ural'sk, he then returned on 1 October to the small family estate of Boldino in Nizhnii-Novgorod province, hoping to concentrate for a while solely on his writing. This second of Pushkin's famous 'Boldino autumns' was shorter but comparatively no less fruitful than the first, three years before in 1830. In scarcely more than five weeks he now finished his *History of Pugachev* (*Исто́рия Пугачёва*), the narrative poem *Angelo* (*А́нджело*), the fairy stories in verse *Tale of the Fisherman and the Little Fish* and *Tale of the Dead Princess...* (*Ска́зка о рыбаке́ и ры́бке, Ска́зка о мёртвой царе́вне и о семи́ богатыря́х*), his free translations of Mickiewicz's ballads 'Budrys and His Sons' (*Бу́дрыс и его́ сыновья́*) and 'The Governor' (*Воево́да*), and several shorter poems. Recent research has called into question the received view that Pushkin also completed *The Queen of Spades* (*Пи́ковая Да́ма*) at Boldino, and occasional suggestions that he found time to work on *The Captain's Daughter* (*Капита́нская до́чка*) should be discounted. There is no doubt, however, that on 6 October he began *The Bronze Horseman* there; and he finished his poetic masterpiece, according to a note on his manuscript, at 5.05 in the morning of 1 November. The surviving drafts bear witness to the careful intensity of the initial stages of composition. They show too that work on what is now Part 2 was astonishingly fluent: condensed, in effect, into only two sleepless nights.

In another respect, however, the poem which Pushkin dashed off in such rapid time alongside competing projects at Boldino had been many years in unconscious gestation. Quite apart from the flood of 1824 – the poem's central episode, of which Pushkin was put in mind by the perilously swelling waters of the Neva as he left Petersburg in August 1833 – his narrative could not have been what it was without his protracted reflections on the Decembrist Revolt of 1825 or the Polish Insurrection of 1830-1 (events which, like the flood of 1824, he learned about only *in absentia*), or on the private circumstance of his marriage to Natal'ia Goncharova in 1831. Nor could it have taken its eventual shape without his previous treatment of 'Petersburg themes' in *The Little House in Kolomna* (*Дóмик в Колóмне*), his unfinished narrative poem *Ezerskii* (*Езéрский*) of 1832-3, or his detailed literary and historical work on Peter the Great. Arguably, of course, it was rooted in the entirety of his previous literary experience. *The Bronze Horseman* was also the product of Pushkin's voracious reading and formidable memory. It reflects his familiarity with conventional literature of every quality and era, from the classical poetry of Ovid to the patriotic doggerel of Count Khvostov, from the odic tradition and family idyll of the eighteenth century to Gothic and Byronic strands of nineteenth-century Romanticism. It also draws substantially on newspapers, journals and propagandistic pamphlets, as well as private letters and conversations, improbable rumours and comic anecdotes. Some of this material is referred to in the Introduction and Notes to the present edition; but it should be emphasised that a good deal besides – self-quotation and fleeting echoes of previous poets, aware-ness of which apparently adds little to the overall meaning of the text, and more conjectural parallels dealt with in specialist studies – has necessarily been left out of account.

Certainly, Pushkin's ability to synthesise and transform the most dis-parate and outwardly incompatible material is one of the hallmarks of *The Bronze Horseman*, and an integral part of the mystery and wonder of its creation: the inspired crystallisation of lengthy experience into the efforts of a few days at Boldino. To most foreign readers on first acquaintance, it is nevertheless far from apparent just why one of Pushkin's shortest narratives, a work of a mere 480 lines, should be quite so highly regarded: for if, as is generally accepted, this is indeed Pushkin's greatest poem, his unrivalled reputation as national poet implies that it must also be one of the finest pieces of poetry ever produced in Russia, and perhaps elsewhere. (The British scholar John Bayley, for instance, writing from a broad European perspective, unequivocally terms *The Bronze Horseman* 'the most remarkable of nineteenth-century poems'.) The rest of this Introduction explores some of the poem's possible significances in the hope of at least pointing towards an explanation. It looks first at poetic form, before turning to some central themes and images, and the vexed questions of meaning and 'message'.

Versification

There is no doubt that one reason for the poem's enduring reputation lies in the sheer technical mastery of Pushkin's mature verse. It is therefore as well to explain at the outset that, like the majority of Pushkin's narrative verse poems and much of his lyric poetry, *The Bronze Horseman* is written throughout in lines of regular four-foot iambic metre (iambic tetrameter). Due in no small measure to Pushkin's own practice, this is the commonest (as well as the most flexible and semantically neutral) of the so-called 'syllabo-tonic' metres in which virtually all classical Russian verse is composed: 'syllabic' in requiring a clearly defined number of syllables per line; 'tonic' in stipulating also that stressed (tonic) syllables may occur only at specific positions within the line. The iamb is simply a two-syllable sequence of unstressed syllable followed by stressed syllable ($\cup$ —). In a line of iambic *tetrameter*, this basic iambic unit, or 'foot', occurs four times. Thus, the metrical basis of *The Bronze Horseman* can be represented as:

$$\cup — | \cup — | \cup — | \cup —$$

And hence, to take an uncomplicated example from the poem:

Черне́|ли из|бы здесь| и та́м.

The syllabo-tonic principle of verse organisation is well-suited to the single stress per word and emphatic differentiation between stressed and unstressed syllables which are inherent characteristics of Russian. Plainly, however, Russian stress does not fall conveniently on every second syllable (statistically it occurs less frequently: every 2.7 or 2.8 – or very roughly once every third syllable); and persistent repetition of any unvarying short sequence of stressed and unstressed syllables would soon prove extremely monotonous. The *metre* of a poem is accordingly a convenient theoretical abstraction. It is realised in practice not through the utterly regular alternation of unstressed and stressed syllables, but through 'rhythmic variations', made possible by the optional *omission* of 'expected' metrical stresses (or 'ictuses'). Only on the final ictus of any line is fulfilment of stress constant and obligatory. The four-stress line quoted above, with stresses on the second, fourth, sixth and eighth syllables (first, second, third and fourth feet or ictuses) is thus only one of the permissible variants of the iambic tetrameter. Many lines of iambic tetrameter instead have three stresses – with non-fulfilment of stress either on the first ictus (i.e. stressing of syllables 4, 6 and 8):

Препоручу́ хозя́йство на́ше ($\cup\cup | \cup — | \cup — | \cup — | \cup$);

on the second ictus (stressing of syllables 2, 6 and 8):

И пе́ной разъярённых во́д ($\cup — | \cup\cup | \cup — | \cup —$);

or on the third ictus (stressing of syllables 2, 4 and 8):

В грани́т оде́лася Нева́ ($\cup — | \cup — | \cup\cup | \cup —$).

And the following line from Pushkin's poem contains just two stresses, on the second and fourth ictus:

Адмиралте́йская игла́   (∪∪│∪ —│∪∪│∪ —).

For reasons which modern verse-theory accounts for in precise detail, the third variant of the three-stress line (with non-fulfilment of stress on the penultimate ictus) is far more common than the other two, and more common even than the four-stress line. The remaining theoretical possibilities for the two-stress line (first and fourth or third and fourth ictus stress) are extremely rare, and do not occur in *The Bronze Horseman*. Neither does the extreme case of the one-stress line.

Though it is the combinatory possibilities of contrasting – or identical – rhythmic variants that essentially determine the rhythmic impetus of a poem, scope for more subtle modulation even within a single variant of a given metre is afforded by such factors as the lengths of words, and whether the breaks between them coincide with, or span, the metrical boundaries between ictuses. So, for example, there is a clearly discernible difference in rhythmic feel between the following two lines, despite the fact that both have three stresses, with an unstressed third ictus:

Пехо́│тных ра́│тей и│ коне́й   (∪ —│∪ —│∪∪│∪ —);
Люблю́│, вое́│нная│ столи́ца   (∪ —│∪ —│∪∪│∪ —│∪).

These secondary factors provide no less than 41 potential rhythmic permutations of the iambic tetrameter. On the other hand, pursuit of rhythmic variety through the inclusion of 'extra' (hypermetrical) stress on metrically weak positions (e.g. the odd syllables of an iambic metre) is not permitted, at least as concerns words of two or more syllables. Apparent exceptions are some two- or three-syllable prepositions and conjunctions; but these less significant parts of speech have at most only weak secondary stress, and are usually considered unstressed for metrical purposes (see, e.g., lines 79, 247 or 350 of Pushkin's text). *Monosyllables* used in weak positions may, however, bear hypermetric stress:

Прошло́ сто́ ле́т, и ю́ный гра́д   (∪ —│— —│∪ —│∪ —).

The poem's metrical inertia is such that the word in question here (сто) is probably rendered less than usually emphatic; but encumbrance of the rhythmic contour through heavier stressing can naturally provide for dramatic articulation, of a kind perhaps more apparent from the following:

Наро́д   (∪ —)
Зри́т Бо́жий гне́в и ка́зни ждёт.   (— —│∪ —│∪ —│∪ —)
Увы́! всё ги́бнет: кро́в и пи́ща!   (∪ —│— —│∪ —│∪ —│∪).

Nevertheless, the overwhelming majority of monosyllables used by Pushkin in *metrically weak* positions are neither verbs nor nouns, but inherently unstressed prepositions, conjunctions or particles (cf. и in the above examples).

The ability to exploit the inherent rhythmic dynamics of the iambic tetrameter was not of course unique to Pushkin. Although his practice determined norms important to the subsequent history of Russian verse, it would be misleading to suggest that, of itself, his handling of the features so far described significantly distinguishes his poem from those of other gifted contemporaries. Awareness of the poem's metrical framework is nevertheless essential to a proper appreciation of Pushkin's achievement; and careful reading in the light of the principles outlined will reveal numerous examples of his subtle rhythmic control. (Note, for instance, such simple effects as the use of a two-stress line to lend finality to the conclusion of a section (e.g. Порфиронóсная вдовá, l. 42); the accumulation of four-stress lines to convey the force of the flood (ll. 190-5, 265-9); or the persistent exploitation of metre to give emphasis to particular words – often in conjunction with the mild syntactic inversion which is a feature of Russian verse rather than prose: Петрá творéнье for творéнье Петрá, etc.) Over longer segments of text, however, rhythmic impetus depends also on the interrelationship of metre with syntax (sentence structure), and on the distribution of rhyme. Here a more distinctive pattern begins to emerge, which distinguishes *The Bronze Horseman* not only from the work of other poets, but also from other works by Pushkin.

The metrical line is so fundamental to the organisation of Russian verse that there is a strong tendency (particularly pronounced in the eighteenth century, gradually less so with the passage of time) for metrical units to coincide with syntactic units: in other words, for the ends of lines to be accompanied by a syntactic break, marking the end of a phrase, clause or sentence. In general, regular observation of 'end-stopping' tends to accentuate the symmetrical contour of the verse, and to create a steady, well-balanced, perhaps stately rhythmic flow. As at the beginning of the following passage, it is often accompanied by other elements of structural symmetry: verbal repetition (particularly at the start of successive lines, where the device is known as anaphora), parallelism of grammatical structures, secondary rhythmic-syntactic division of individual lines into equal halves (hemistiches), and so forth. This, too, readily contributes towards a measured, somewhat formal or rhetorical rhythmico-intonational pattern:

Люблю́ тебя́, Петрá творéнье,
Люблю́ твой стрóгий, стрóйный вид,
Невы́ держáвное течéнье,
Береговóй её гранúт,
Твоúх огрáд узóр чугýнный,

Твои́х заду́мчивых ноче́й
Прозра́чный су́мрак, блеск безлу́нный...

End-stopping is nevertheless dispensed with in the penultimate line quoted, where an *enjambement* occurs: the sense (syntax) is carried over into the following line. This divergence from the clause-length regularly maintained over the five previous lines indicates another potentially rich source of rhythmic variation. Here, the enjambement is accentuated by placement of the 'delayed' syntactic break in the middle rather than at the end of the next line, although a subtle interplay of contrasting processes simultaneously attenuates its effect: the disruptive jerk of the enjambement is combined with an emphatically symmetrical ordering resulting from anaphoric repetition of Твои́х. The tension between harmonious formal pattern and potential chaotic dissolution recurs at every level of the poem, and has profound thematic importance.

Elsewhere, enjambement naturally lends itself to a variety of expressive effect. Its deflection of attention from the formal boundary of the verse line makes it well-suited to less 'poetic', more colloquial or prosaic passages, in which structural parallelisms are relatively few, and there is approximation to the rhythms of ordinary speech. One example are the repeated enjambements during the lengthy introduction of Evgenii at the beginning of Part 1 (ll. 108-44), beginning with the extreme case of a line-break between pronoun and accompanying verb (Оно́/Звучи́т прия́тно). This is so remote from what is usually considered to 'sound pleasant', that the discrepancy between stated meaning and formal device constitutes one of several ironies underpinning the section's unconventional chatter. Though recourse to enjambement was well established by Pushkin's day, however, what is particularly striking about *The Bronze Horseman* is not just its aptness and dazzling success in many isolated instances (as to convey Evgenii's disequilibrium in ll. 348-74, or the chaotic disruption and obliteration of familiar contours caused by the flood in ll. 182-9 and 293-311), but the sheer frequency of its occurrence. Andrew Kahn calculates that enjambement is employed in more than 40% of lines, as compared to significantly below 30% in others of Pushkin's own narrative poems (Kahn, p. 36). The implication is that, whatever the associated stylistic or intonational tendencies, lines or short groups of lines with and without enjambement are in practice closely interwoven throughout the poem. The point could be illustrated by virtually any random segment, including the solemn introductory panegyric to St Petersburg partially quoted above; it is nowhere more striking than in the complex rhythmic modulations from enjambement to end-stopping and back again in connection with the transitions between nervous febrility and awesome grandeur in the passage where Evgenii recognises the statue in Part 2 (ll. 404-23). But the use of enjambement in something approaching half the lines of the poem – supplemented, incidentally, by the incidence of an 'internal' full-stop in roughly a third of lines – points also to a radical innovation on Pushkin's part: not so much a subversion of the integrity of the line, as an unprecedented expansion and liberation beyond the accepted rhythmic confines of the iambic tetrameter.

A comparable process characterises Pushkin's use of rhyme. In one respect, the poem's rhymes are entirely conventional. It will be noted that while many of Pushkin's lines of iambic tetrameter have eight syllables, as many again contain nine, with an 'extra', unstressed syllable after the obligatory stress on the final ictus. The former, with final stress, are said to have a masculine ending or 'clausula'; the latter, with final unstressed syllable, have feminine clausula. Lines with the same clausula are combined together in rhyming pairs or sometimes triplets, Russian rhyme being based on identity (or near-identity) of sound *from the last stressed vowel onwards*: thus по́лн/во́лн, широ́ко/одино́ко, etc. Masculine rhymes ending in a single vowel (but not a diphthong: e.g. поле́й/коне́й) also require identity of the preceding supporting consonant (сужденó/окнó, корабли́/земли́). Other rhymes may often contain some optional element of enrichment through comparable 'leftward' identity of supporting consonants and/or vowels (e.g. волна́м/к на́м, or вода́ми/сада́ми, where the pronunciation of unstressed 'o' as 'a' increases the identity; there are also some more complex instances, of the type: ба́лов/бока́лов, сто́й/с тобо́й, же дру́жно/ не ну́жно, etc.).

Like the majority of narrative poems of its time, *The Bronze Horseman* is written not in regular stanzas with fixed rhyme scheme, but in free-rhyming sections or verse paragraphs of varying length. Masculine and feminine rhymes alternate invariably throughout (with the exception of three unrhymed lines: see note to l. 183); but the rhyme sequence is otherwise not predetermined. The basic units are quatrains of alternating (abab) and of enclosed rhyme (abba), and couplets (aa) or, more frequently, quatrains of adjacent rhyme (aabb). These may appear in any combination, with further scope for variety arising from an occasional switch from pairs to three-line rhyming units (abaab, etc.). Quite apart from the inherent propensity of rhyme to emphasise significant words, the flexibility and unpredictability of this arrangement naturally lends itself to all manner of expressive effects. Several instances are described in the Notes (e.g. to ll. 1-14, 92, 188-9, 259, etc.). As with metre, however, the strikingly distinctive feature of Pushkin's rhyming is in the interplay with syntactic structures. In Pushkin's earlier work, as in that of his contemporaries, there is a strong tendency for the ends of rhyming sequences to coincide with and mark the ends of syntactic-semantic units. In *The Bronze Horseman*, this is often not the case. The extreme example comes at the end of the poem, where the full stop that brings the work to a close concludes an indivisible twenty-six line sequence, initiated by the phrase И с той поры́... (l. 456), during which the boundaries between sentences and rhyming units do not once coincide. While much shorter, two- and four-line rhyming-syntactic chains do of course occur, there is another sequence of nineteen lines, spanning a boundary between verse paragraphs (ll. 260-78), and others commonly extend to fourteen, fifteen or sixteen lines. The effect is of a remarkable freedom in the handling of the verse, of the creation of unprecedented space within the narrow confines of the tetrameter, while the resistance to separation into easily digestible, discrete units, enables an unusual complexity of discourse, a density and intensity of thought which requires sustained concentration on the part of the reader. Like the tension of symmetry and disorder referred to above, the combination of certainty (the recurrence inherent in rhyme) and uncertainty (when will the sequence end?) arguably has its counterpart also on a higher semantic level.

One final aspect of Pushkin's technique which merits attention here is his orchestration of sound. The Symbolist poet Valerii Briusov argued with great eloquence that the organisation of sound was of exceptional importance in the composition of Pushkin's verse, and did much to explain its unique appeal. Pushkin's poetry was 'a complex but completely regulated pattern of sound', in which 'every line was considered from a euphonic point of view..., every letter took its place with reference to the sound which it conveys', and phonetics were invariably an important factor in the choice of words (Briusov, p. 128). This tendency reached its apogee in *The Bronze Horseman*. The practical consequence is well illustrated by a modern critic, A.D.P. Briggs, who writes of the two famous lines already quoted:

Люблю́ тебя́, Петра́ творе́нье,
Люблю́ твой стро́гий, стро́йный вид:

...the ultimate effect depends on intricate multiple uses of those gentle consonants 'l', 'p' and 't' with just a touch of strength imparted by an occasionally interpolated 'r' and a sudden 'g' in the second line; ...the straightforward repetition of 'str' in that line has been partly anticipated by the 'tr' in 'Petra', the two letters being repeated, though slightly separated, in 'tvoren'ye'; ...the sound of 'Petra' was itself foreshadowed in ghostly fashion by 'tebya'; ...the unrelated 'tvoy' relates back in sound to 'tvoren'ye', and so on *ad nauseam*.
(Briggs, 1990, p. 50; one might easily add, for instance, that the 'b's interwoven between repeated 'l's are closely related to 'p'
– as voiced and unvoiced variants of a labial consonant).

The essential point, however, is that this intricate acoustic structure is by no means exceptional. Pushkin does not merely resort to expressive effect at particular moments, from the near-onomatopoeic alliteration which renders the fizzy sparkling of champagne (Шипе́нье пе́нистых бока́лов/И пу́нша пла́мень голубо́й) to the clamour of the horses hooves in the famous scene of Evgenii's pursuit: the main characteristic of the poem's phonic organisation is the virtually unfailing presence of a less obtrusive but astonishingly intricate patterning of precisely the type outlined by Briggs. The assertion can be verified only by exhaustive analysis (but take, for instance, the three 'v's, three 'n's, three 't's [t- unvoiced d-t] of an entirely unremarkable line such as Свой ве́тхий не́вод, ны́не там, amplified by the sequence 've', 'ne', 'ne', the reversal of 've' in the 'ev' of the following word, etc.). The result is a verbal texture of extraordinary yet subtle density. It makes the poem both melodic and memorable (sound patterning, like rhythmic patterning, is in part a mnemonic device), and fittingly complements the density of thought and image which is the more evident cause of its enduring success.

Major Themes

Even a cursory reading of *The Bronze Horseman* reveals thematic preoccupations of considerable, perhaps intractable complexity. Central to the latter part of the narrative is a conflict – or more precisely, an inescapable non-convergence of interests – between the private individual and the state: specifically the autocratic Russian state created by Peter I, and perpetuated by successors including Catherine the Great, Alexander I and Nicholas I; but perhaps also, in a more general sense, any large-scale, modern, impersonal political system. For all the emotional sympathy the individual might attract – the petty government clerk or 'little man' who was rapidly to become a major preoccupation of Russian literature, but perhaps also the 'ordinary citizen' anywhere – it seems inevitable that the needs of the state and the common good should outweigh the claims of isolated individuals. To condemn the state (or its leaders) for pursuing its grand designs might seem tantamount either to implicitly condoning revolution, or to an obscurantist rejection of any possibility of consciously-directed 'change from above'. Yet to withhold condemnation may be to sanction private misery. One of the complex moral issues underlying the plot is thus the human cost of social progress, economic prosperity and enlightenment: is state developent to be rejected if it entails the suffering of individual members?

The state itself, however, is less resilient than might first appear. Another major narrative strand concerns its vulnerability to natural forces, and hence the potential fragility of human endeavour and transience of historical time. This leads to fundamental considerations of whether or not our existence is ordered, purposeful and meaningful: whether our lives are guided by Divine Providence or Fate, or instead chaotic, random and absurd. On a less cosmic scale, Pushkin's poem also prompts speculation as to the peculiar identity and true essence of Russia, poised between East and West; and calls into question whether the Imperial Russia created by Peter, through its break with Orthodox tradition and its engenderment of a discontented under-class, bears inherently within itself the seeds of its own destruction. A more prominent stimulus to thought is the paradoxical (and profoundly symbolic) nature of Peter's city of St Petersburg, at once both elegantly, dazzlingly beautiful, and dark and terrible; rich and squalid; rationally conceived, yet the focus of irrational forces and events. In literary terms, while synthesising previous writing, *The Bronze Horseman* was in this respect the source of a distinctive and remarkably productive 'Petersburg theme'. Numerous writers from Gogol' and Dostoevskii to Andrei Belyi and Anna Akhmatova followed Pushkin's lead in using the city's imposing facade as a backdrop to themes of madness, destruction and the demonic, and contemplation of the uncertain boundaries of reality.

The endless fascination of the poem, however, stems not solely from the range and profundity of the issues it compresses into fewer than 500 short (eight- or nine-syllable!) lines, but from the manner of their treatment. It is not true, as is sometimes suggested, that Pushkin is non-judgmental: instead, he is prone to subvert every fixed conception, to undermine every assumption and de-stabilise every point of view including his own (or that of his narrator). The most obvious example is the disconcerting discontinuity between the two aspects of St Petersburg just referred to: between the enthusiastic, eulogistic tone of the Introduction and the gloom of the 'Petersburg Tale' which follows. Though it is difficult to reconcile the two, it would be an arbitrary over-simplification to take either one as the definitive picture – Pushkin's final word on St Petersburg. The same holds true over shorter segments of text. Thus, for example, the overtly sustained praise of the Introduction is arguably compromised, on the one hand, by the combination of aesthetic appreciation with military and mercantile considerations (Pushkin's contempt for tradesmen was made clear in several poems, as well as in the brief passage at lines 339-43), and by chauvinistic political sentiment. And Pushkin's expression of love for St Petersburg is also, as it were, under-mined from within, by a series of submerged anomalies, some of which are described in the Notes. Repeatedly, the lack of a single, stable focus renders the poem's meaning exceptionally complex and elusive, to the extent that it is even difficult – without recounting the plot at considerable length – to say exactly what *The Bronze Horseman* is about. To account in more detail for this resistance to unitary interpretation, it will be convenient to look in turn at the central images of Peter, Evgenii, and the flood.

Peter

Peter the Great (1672-1725) provides a more effective touchstone than any other figure in pre-Revolutionary Russian history for consideration of the socio-political and even philosophical issues referred to above. In simplified terms which are entirely appropriate to the context of *The Bronze Horseman*, Peter achieved a radical break with the traditional Russian world of Old Muscovy – religious-minded, elaborately ritualistic, semi-Asiatic, mistrustful of change and suspicious of foreign influence. He could be said single-handedly to have transformed his country into a strong, westward looking, modern, imperialistic European power, predominantly secular rather than religious; and his newly created capital of St Petersburg seemed compellingly emblematic of the dramatic changes he had wrought. Yet the far-reaching success of his reforms derived from his unlimited autocratic authority as much as from his boundless personal energy and strong will. St Petersburg was built by the forced labour of many thousands of poorly equipped peasant conscripts, who lived and died in atrocious conditions. It was even populated under duress. Development was inseparable from despotism, and depended in no small measure on coercion and brutality. In the eyes of his supporters Peter performed glorious deeds of unparalleled grandeur; to his fiercest opponents, it was not merely a matter of the end failing to justify the means, but of sacrilegious usurpation of Orthodox Russia's unique, God-given national identity.

Naturally, Pushkin was not the first Russian man of letters who felt drawn to evaluate the achievements of Peter the Great; and *The Bronze Horseman* is only one reflection of his own abiding fascination with Peter's reign. His most substantial previous treatments had resulted in two contrasting, though comparably idealised portraits of the tsar: as private family-man, simple, practical and approachable in *The Negro of Peter the Great* (*Арап Петра Великого*, 1827); and as public figurehead – victorious general, statesman and national hero in the long narrative poem, *Poltava* (*Полтава*, 1828). In 1831, Pushkin had also embarked, with the permission and encouragement of Nicholas I, on an official *History of Peter I* (*История Петра Первого*). This involved extensive research in state archives, and although never completed, occupied Pushkin increasingly during the last years of his life. By the time he began *The Bronze Horseman*, his knowledge of Peter's reign was therefore both immensely detailed and unusually privileged. It is worth bearing in mind, too, that Pushkin's 'professional' literary-historical interest in Peter had a personal underside, which was itself symptomatically double-edged. In one respect, Pushkin's family had literally originated with Peter's direct blessing. The 'Negro' of Peter the Great was Pushkin's own maternal great-grandfather, who had been given to Peter as a young captive: Peter became his god-father when he converted to Orthodoxy in 1707, and launched him on a long and successful military career. By contrast, one of Pushkin's ancestors on his father's side had been condemned to death by Peter for allegedly plotting against him. Fedor Matveevich Pushkin perished in 1697, in a gruesome execution carried out to Peter's precise instructions.

It is typical of the oblique methods which enable Pushkin to engender multiple meanings that Peter the Great, who so dominates *The Bronze Horseman*, is nevertheless characterised largely *in absentia*, through his works, reputation – and posthumous representation as bronze statue. He is properly present only for the first twenty lines – and ten of these are taken up by public thoughts, recorded in first person plural, мы form. Peter plainly emerges from these few lines as an ambitious and belligerent head of state, but the political dimension seems of relative insignificance compared to the mere fact of his imposing presence: his nameless solitude, the scope of his vision, and the grandeur and mystery with which he is endowed. The 'great thoughts' which 'fill' him are in stark contrast to the emptiness of the remote wilderness which surrounds him, and the capitalised pronoun Он which is his sole designation accentuates his awesome stature. It is as if he transcends the ordinary, mortal need for identification by name; and some critics have seen here an implicit parallel to the Old Testament God, whose name may not be taken in vain. Certainly the implication of a God-like being might be detected in the lines that follow, where the abstraction of Peter's 'far-sighted' thought (даль in l. 3 obviously suggests time as well as space) acquires triumphantly concrete realisation. It is not simply that 'huts' have given way to 'palaces', 'marshes' to 'gardens', 'poor' and solitary 'small boats' to a 'crowd' of grand ships at 'rich piers'; Peter's act of creation (Петра творенье, l. 43) is a superhuman, even 'miraculous' (l. 436) transformation, and Pushkin describes it in terms which recall fundamental cosmogonical or creation myths.

In different ways, many such myths record the emergence of 'Cosmos' (form, or manifested being) from 'Chaos' – the primordial substance, vast, dark and godless: in its original meaning simply 'gap' or 'void'; but also 'confusion' and, specifically, the formless mass in which the 'elements' (earth, air, fire and water – all notably recurrent images of Pushkin's poem) were scattered through space. One readily accessible account of this creative process comes at the start of Ovid's *Metamorphoses* – which Pushkin knew well, and perhaps alludes to at a later stage of *The Bronze Horseman* (see ll. 188-9 and note). In the beginning, according to Ovid:

> ...Nature presented the same aspect the world over, that to
> which men have given the name of Chaos. This was a shapeless
> uncoordinated mass...whose ill-assorted elements were indis-

criminately [cf. Pushkin's здесь и там?] heaped together in one place. There was no sun, in those days, to provide the world with light [cf. спрятанное со́лнце].... Although the elements of land and air and sea were there, the earth had no firmness, the water no fluidity [cf. то́пи блат, neither water nor earth], there was no brightness in the sky. Nothing had any lasting shape, but everything got in the way of everything else....

This was finally resolved by a god, a natural force of a higher kind, who separated the earth from the heaven and the waters from the earth, and set the clear air apart from the cloudy atmosphere. When he had freed these elements, sorting them out from the heap where they had lain,...he bound them fast, each in its separate place, forming a harmonious union.*

This is broadly comparable to the Biblical creation described in the Book of Genesis, to which critics of Pushkin have sometimes referred:

And the earth was without form and void: and darkness *was* upon the face of the deep. And the Spirit of God moved upon the face of the waters
And God said, Let there be light: and there was light...and God divided the light from the darkness... (Genesis, 1:2-4).

Perhaps, indeed, the mythical status which Pushkin seems to attribute to Peter as god-like creator carries appropriate overtones of both traditions. Peter's state was neither wholly pagan nor wholly Christian, but combined elements of both; and the intertwining of pagan (Classical) and Christian motifs, involving multiple coincidences and divergences, forms an ideologically complex substratum throughout the poem.

The 'beauty and wonder' with which Peter's mental conception is endowed as it takes 'strict and harmonious' (l. 44) form from indiscriminate shapelessness is also projected against a sharp temporal transition between 'then' and 'now' (пре́жде/ны́не). The darkness (including the fog, and the blackness of the randomly scattered huts) has given way to light, to the extent that the new city scarcely knows the night (ll. 55-8). The uncoordinated horizontal plane of the opening, with its 'wide', featureless expanse, is replaced by the vertical soar of buildings, spires and, eventually, statue (the same vertical perspective will be carried through to Evgenii's confrontations with the Bronze Horseman), and the once soft, marshy absence of 'lasting shape' has ceded to the hard contours of well-patterned structures, clearly delimited within durable boundaries of granite and cast iron. In more abstract terms, Peter's imposition of formal structure has brought a

*Ovid, *Metamorphoses*, trans. Mary M. Innes, Penguin, 1955, p. 29.

sense of history, national identity and civilisation to a realm previously inhabited by 'nature's' (rather than organised culture's?) 'poor stepsons' (l. 26) – the 'miserable', isolated, a-historical Finns. Linear, historical time now takes apparent precedence over cyclical, natural time (cf. ll. 21, 81-3 and note), and from a realm at the remote periphery of existence, the city becomes a centre, a focal point for commerce 'from all the ends of the earth' (l. 33). The god-like scale of Peter's accomplishment is further underscored by another of the antitheses introduced in the opening lines and developed later in the poem: that between wood and stone. (In order to concentrate scarce resources on the capital, in 1714 Peter had outlawed building in stone anywhere else in Russian, thereby enshrining the distinction in law.) Not only is the city of stone which ostensibly bears his name founded by Peter, he is in a mythical sense the foundation and very substance upon which it is built: his unnamed name derives from *petra*, the Greek word for rock – Jesus's epithet for Peter the first apostle, the 'rock' or 'stone' (in Russian, ка́мень) upon which He built his church (Matthew, 16:18). Secondary associations therefore evoke the Apostle Peter's Holy City of Rome, the once undisputed centre and capital of the Christian world, as of the pagan world before it. The contrasting imagery of wood links the Finnish forests and black huts of the first lines not only with Evgenii and Parasha's home, but also, perhaps, with non-Petrine, non-rationally conceived Moscow – the city with which the poem's opening section, beginning with the primordial Finnish Gulf, comes to a slightly unexpected close (ll. 40-2).

While the grand rhetorical sweep of the Introduction may seem endorsement enough of Peter's endeavour, shorter poems by Pushkin suggest he felt a special affinity with Peter precisely as fellow creator. It is the task of the poet, too, to create out of nothingness, clothing his 'thoughts' in strict and harmonious form, fixing the promptings of mental vision within confining boundaries – albeit of rhyme and metre rather than stone and metal. The poet is a tsar in his solitary creative freedom ('To the Poet' [Поэ́ту], 1830); and Pushkin's description of Peter plunged in thought at the beginning of *The Bronze Horseman* has a striking analogue in his evocation of literary creation in 'The Poet' (Поэ́т, 1827). There the poet is the most insignificant of beings, until he is transformed by divine inspiration, and hastens to a landscape re-encountered in the narrative poem: the 'shores of desolate waves' (На берега́ пусты́нных волн) and 'resonant' forests of oak (широкошу́мные дубро́вы; cf. лес...Круго́м шуме́л, in *The Bronze Horseman*, ll. 9-11). Though the lyric poem ends at this point, the inspirational communion with primordial nature, like Peter's, will evidently be translated into elegant structure. The penultimate rhyme of полн/волн (a favourite of Pushkin's 'creative' pieces, which confirms the connection with *The Bronze Horseman*) is anticipated in the sequence Аполло́н/сон/он at the outset: Apollo, the god of light and poetry, is also the deity of construction and plastic form. And just as Peter created an enduring memorial to his name, so Pushkin intended that his work, too, should live on as a permanent monument to himself: as he put it in 'The Monument' (Памятник, 1836), that it should soar higher than Alexander's Column (вознестись; cf. l. 24 of *The Bronze Horseman*) – St Petersburg's newest statue to a tsar, and evidently a less worthy counterpart to the poet than Peter.

There is an obvious rightness to *The Bronze Horseman's* implicit parallel between the tsar who might be considered the founder of the modern Russian state and the poet who, with comparable justification, might be regarded as the fountainhead of modern Russian literature. The potential arrogance of Pushkin's proud self-identification with Peter is doubtless attenuated by its obliqueness; but what is most important in Pushkin is often most deeply submerged, and there is perhaps another sense in which the poet has the upper hand. The tsar at the beginning of *The Bronze Horseman* arguably *gains* in dignity through implicit comparison to the poet-creator, rather than vice versa; and *this* Peter – the Peter of the poem, who, for instance, can think thoughts articulated by an Italian philosopher some years after his death (see Pushkin's first footnote) – is firmly the creation of Pushkin. Even Tsars have their human place; and amid the poem's many themes, we should not forget its importance as a literary 'monument' of the author's.

In more obvious ways, too, for all Pushkin's admiration and empathy, his portrait of Peter is by no means unambiguously positive. In the first place, 'Peter's creation' is less untarnished than the radiant picture of the Introduction would suggest. From the first lines of Part 1 onward, his city becomes transformed into a place of darkness and sorrow. It is a telling detail that the 'window' we now encounter is no inlet for Western enlightenment, but Evgenii's flimsy defence against the harsh assault of the gloomy elements (l. 162; contrast l. 16). Peter's city may have arisen 'magnificently and proudly' (l. 24) on the very margins of the habitable world, but as the waters swell – and coffins are washed down the streets – its vulnerability becomes increasingly apparent. Like Peter's statue, it seems poised precariously over the abyss (chaos, the void), hovering on the threshold between being and oblivion. The extent of its (im)permanence must be taken up below, but there is plainly as much cause to doubt the judgement of a tsar who determined to build под морем (l. 413) as to marvel at his daring. Perhaps, indeed, the man of 'vision' (l. 3) and calculating purpose failed to foresee the true consequences of his wilful acts? The famous apostrophe to tsar and galloping steed as the poem nears its end (ll. 418-23) projects these doubts from past and present into the future (Где опустишь...?), and from the fate of the city to the destiny of the entire nation-state which Peter created. Is the horseman truly in command of the rearing beast he has stirred into such dynamic life, or powerless to avert impending disaster? Despite the unsettling paradoxes that the tsar is long dead and his mount an immobile statue of bronze, should the climactic invocation of Peter as мóщный властелúн судьбы́ therefore be taken to express unstinting awe or profound irony?

As the Notes indicate in more detail, there is also scope for more fanci-fully symbolic interpretation. Though Peter may seem God-like, he is not God – or even, as Ovid put it, 'a god, a natural force' – but perhaps all-too-human. In this respect, his creation out of nothing could be regarded as the height of human presumption: an attempt to mimic and usurp the true Creator. His self-reliant arrogance is emphasised by his name's association both with St Petersburg and the 'stone' from which it is constructed, with the implication of a place made in the tsar's own mortal image (on the blasphemous connotations of 'graven imagery' see also note to l. 259); and this sacrilegious act of self-idolatry would render Peter directly responsible for the flood – an expression of divine wrath, ineluctably visited upon his impious creation (see e.g. l. 200). The flood might even evoke the End of time, and Peter's equestrian statue the fourth horseman of the Apocalypse, whose emergence before the Final Judgement heralds the 'great day' of God's wrath: 'his name...was Death, and Hell followed with him' (Revela-tion, 6: 8,17; cf. the 'abyss' over which Peter's horse is poised?). Alterna-tively, Peter's construction from the void may be regarded as a form of unholy magic, and thus, as the narrative unfolds, it becomes increasingly apparent that his city, like his statue, bears only a spectral semblance of life; in essence, he has brought forth a nether kingdom of death (ll. 285-96 and note). Typically, Pushkin gives grounds for such interpretations and apparently dispels them as melodramatic exaggeration, only to leave fresh hints at a later point in the narrative. They are ostensibly subverted, but their symbolic resonances never quite abandoned.

In addition to the (human) fallibility which might compromise Peter's image, there is also his (literally 'inhuman'?) cruelty. This is hinted at from the outset, in his decision to build a city на зло – to spite not an 'enemy' but a 'neighbour', for whom, plainly, he has not a glimmer of Christian love or charity. Covert hints of darker deeds apart (see, e.g., notes to ll. 75-6 and footnote 1), his cruelty is next implied in the form of the impassive indifference of a powerful despot, who might seem to turn his back on the tribulations of ordinary people (l. 255 and note) and, if he *did* foresee the consequences of his creative endeavour, must have knowingly incorporated suffering into his scheme of things. In Part 2, however, haughty indiffer-ence gives way to active malevolence. The bringer of light and civilisation is now framed in darkness and filled with fire. In the inert form of the monstrous 'idol' (кумúр, истукáн), he is revealed in his most 'dread' aspect, as he (it) stirs to uncanny life (the demonic power over death, again?), to gallop in vengeful pursuit of a single, weak, discontented individual. This is a vindictive tyrant, chillingly characterised by the 'iron bridle' (l. 422) through which he wields power over the symbolic Russian steed.

And yet, of course, the statue does not trample Evgenii underfoot. He is not caught and killed, and this is perhaps only one way in which Peter's cruelty is mitigated. It could even be reasoned – however harshly – that the 'proud idol's' subjugation of Evgenii is justifiable: at worst a necessary evil, essential to preserve the stability and victorious might which Pushkin's Introduction so vigorously endorses, and to maintain Russian (or Romanov?) dominion over 'half the world' (l. 427). In a quite different respect, the reader is also left to decide whether the 'cruel' pursuit of Evgenii has any substantial reality at all: whether it should be taken seriously, or dismissed as the deluded imagining of a deranged mind. This in turn relates to a more fundamental difficulty in assessing Pushkin's 'Peter': for the name of Peter which Pushkin carefully avoids in directly denotative form bears a composite, multi-faceted significance (man, tsar, builder, statue, state; good/evil, heroic/ fallible, living/dead/ slumbering/demonically 'un-dead'). It is an elusive term for a predominantly 'absent' figure, and may or may not be taken to denote a coherently unified entity, or to possess an authentic relation to historical reality. Is there, for instance, really a sufficient continuity between the majestic figure of the opening (itself, perhaps, not so much the 'real' Peter as a fictionalised image, made in the likeness of the poet) and the created city of stone which bears Peter's name and imprint, to allow meaningful judge-ment of the one in terms of the other? Or between 'living' (or deceased) man and 'proud idol'? Is it proper to confound Peter with his posthumous representation as pagan statue (the subjective image of another artist, which *appears* to take on objective existence)? Or to base any judgement of tsar and national destiny on the illusion of dynamic motion created by an immobile statue of solid bronze on stone – until, that is, the statute does after all spring to life and motion (or not, as the case may be!)? The negative rhetorical question (Не так ли?) which concludes the famous apostrophe of the horseman in tentative speculation rather than categorical assertion seems entirely apt. Pushkin's portrayal of Peter gives rise to potentially intractable problems concerning the relation between art and reality, 'real' man and historical process, which are ultimately bound up also with the construction and meaning of meaning.

It is somewhat more readily apparent, however, that final judgement of Peter's complex role is nevertheless inextricably connected to our assess-ment of Evgenii and the flood. We must now turn to the first of these.

Evgenii

At first sight, the role of the 'contemporary', private figure of Evgenii is relatively uncomplicated. Both as a citizen of St Petersburg and as a lowly member of the civil service which Peter established, Evgenii is a creature of Peter. As events take their course, he is also his victim. Evgenii's initial circumstances are straitened, but his aspirations are as modest as his means. He is prepared to work in order to marry, and he dreams of an unassuming domestic contentment with his beloved Parasha and future family. The flood intervenes, and Evgenii, through no fault of his own, loses not only his Parasha, but also his reason. He becomes a social outcast, wandering at random until he once more chances across the statue of Peter, which (or whom!), in a moment of clarity (ll. 404-5), he now 'recognises' as the source of his tragic woes. At the climax of a lengthy passage – perhaps, indeed, of the entire poem – he confronts and challenges the statue of the dread potentate. The horseman's response is ruthless, and Evgenii is put to flight. He dies thereafter, on an abandoned island, on the threshold of the washed-up hut.

Evgenii's poignant fate should command the utmost sympathy, and serve as a damning indictment of the autocratic power – perhaps any system of government – that sacrifices the welfare of the private individual to the broader interests of state. Yet no less than the introductory protestations of love for St Petersburg, Pushkin's forthright expression of compassion for 'our hero' (l. 108):

Но бе́дный, бе́дный мой Евге́ний...

might perhaps by now be expected to alert to a contrary undercurrent of more complex meaning. The moral and intellectual responses prompted by closer consideration of Evgenii, particularly in the light of inevitable comparison and contrast with Peter, indeed prove challengingly intricate.

The first indication that the unfortunate 'little man' may not, after all, deserve unqualified sympathy comes with the initial description of his name and lineage. If Evgenii might belong to an ancient (i.e. Muscovite) family whose fortunes have declined, then in this respect too he might be presumed a hapless victim of the radical social reforms instituted by Peter (see notes to ll. 115, 225-7). There is, moreover, a parallel with Pushkin himself, who in his bitterly ironic poem 'My Genealogy' (Моя́ родосло́вная, 1830) had lamented his own family's decline from eminence in the days of Alexander Nevskii and Ivan IV, and described himself as the 'remnant' (обло́мок) of a lineage in its dotage. The basis for empathy between author and hero might seem all the greater in view of their deliberate remoteness from the aristocrats (знать) of the present: Evgenii shuns them; the author of 'My Genealogy' dismisses them as unworthy parvenus. The difference in underlying attitude is nevertheless telling. Evgenii is unconcernedly forgetful of his forbears, and behaves with self-effacing timidity (ll. 120-1). Pushkin – the professional historian – is acutely mindful of his ancestry, and speaks out with proudly contemptuous scorn. A more obvious disparity, grounded squarely within the text of *The Bronze Horseman*, confirms that Evgenii's lack of interest in a matter of undoubted importance to Pushkin should indeed be considered reprehensible. Peter creates history from nothingness, founding a new historical state. Evgenii ignores even family history, and as the poem progresses, increasingly regresses from the realm of history into an a-temporal void. His death presumably signals the final discontinuation of his family's historical line. If Peter is too illustrious to require a name, Evgenii, in his own display of indifference – arguably, his own pre-emptive version of Peter's turning his back (l. 255) upon the achievement and concerns of his future antagonist! – might seem unworthy to bear one.

If Evgenii is found wanting in his irresponsible approach to the past, he arguably fares little better in relation to present and future. He is of course excluded from Petersburg's social elite; but for all Pushkin's subsequent use of the adjective бедный, he is at the outset very far from the lowest of the low: no destitute beggar, dependent upon charity, or needful of compassion. Although he might wish for more money and brains and feel wistfully envious of those 'happy idlers' who are not obliged to work at all for their living, in truth, he may have little to complain of. He himself has worked for just two years, and in only 'a year or two' more has every prospect of achieving the necessary 'independence' to realise his dream of comfortable stability, with wife, home, household, and children.

Ethical evaluation of such mundane domestic bliss was another issue of personal consequence to Pushkin. From his earliest contemplation of the marriage he eventually contracted in 1831, he had been much preoccupied with the possibility and worth of family happiness. Albeit to the predations of Nicholas I's court rather than to natural disaster, he had later also become increasingly fearful of losing his beloved. If Pushkin doubtless identified himself in part with Peter, there are in other words further equally clear connections between his private circumstances and the terms used to describe the aspirations of his lowly hero (see, e.g., notes to ll. 130, 360). Previously, however, in *The Negro of Peter the Great* or his 'Little Tragedy' *Mozart and Salieri* (*Моцарт и Сальери*. Boldino, 1830), Pushkin had fleetingly contemplated the banal concerns of domesticity as a trait of the man of unrivalled genius. In *The Bronze Horseman* the two spheres are utterly dissociated. The difference in magnitude between Peter and the domestic-minded Evgenii, subtly underlined by many parallels and contrasts (see, e.g., note to l. 127), can scarcely fail to accentuate the paltriness of Evgenii's small-scale vision – which, moreover, in pathetic contrast to Peter's grandiose project, never achieves realisation. And this is the nub of the matter: for Evgenii's very ordinariness, his thoroughly 'average' ambitions and limitations, paradoxically heighten the moral dilemmas which the poem presents. Just as to blame Peter or the state for Evgenii's predicament is, if taken to its logical conclusion, ultimately to imply that any striving for progress, for national power and prosperity, is reprehensible, so to admit any even partial qualification of sympathy for Evgenii, let alone an element of contempt for his modest, petty-bourgeois aspirations, is to adopt the seemingly no less untenable position of human indifference – and ultimately to mimic the despot's disregard for the humdrum rights of the private individual.

Evgenii's dramatic transition from expectation of comfortable attainment to devastating loss might in any case seem to necessitate a revision of attitude. Even here, however, it may be difficult to view his position with total sympathy. Evgenii's fevered anticipation and subsequent shocked discovery that Parasha's hut is gone cause him to lose both his mind (he immediately assumes the worst, apparently never seeking to confirm that Parasha had indeed perished along with her hut) and his place in the Petersburg urban community. His hopes dashed, his life ruined, he becomes a pitiful figure – or rather, we should note, an object of compassion for some, of ridicule and abuse for others (ll. 364-72). He so renounces his existence and identity that he no longer even seems fully human ('ни зверь ни человéк': cf. ll. 376-8). Yet Evgenii is perhaps alone in reacting to the general calamity in this way. For others the flood is not the End they may have previously anticipated. They cope with their losses and get on with their lives, so that by the following day the city already returns from chaos to the uncharitable 'normality' of its 'former order' (l. 334). While this may seem repugnant, an alternative, unspoken but heartless implication is that Evgenii's ab-normal, dis-ordered reaction is somehow misguidedly excessive. After all, if everyone were to surrender so completely to the pain of inescapable grief and loss, humanity might achieve very little: perhaps, indeed, there could be no progress beyond the sorry, meagre lot of the a-historical Finns.

The unsympathetic force of this morally uncomfortable rationalisation is not diminished by closer consideration of why, precisely, Evgenii goes mad. The usual critical assumption is that his insanity reveals his boundless love for Parasha. This would tend to endow him with an increased dignity: despite his unglamorous circumstances, his insanity may be the lofty if conventional response of the noble, hyper-sensitive hero of Romantic literature. The objection is that Pushkin's introduction of Evgenii gives no more evidence of ardent erotic passion than of fiery social resentment. The lengthy passage describing his thoughts – which portrays the common (rather than Romantically exclusive), slightly self-pitying, far from rebellious tendency to bemoan half-heartedly the less-than-perfect circumstances of life – is shot through with cautious reasoning and timidly attenuative qualifications (Что ведь есть; всего; что едвá ли; Дни нà два, нà три; зачéм же нет?; Но что ж?). Parasha, moreover, seems far from the all-consuming focus of Evgenii's attention: it is notable, perhaps, that she appears in his 'stream of consciousness' only after thoughts of self, job, socio-economic betters and worsening weather. Evgenii seemingly regards the prospect of a 'day or two's' separation from her with casual equanimity, and contemplates marriage almost as an after-thought: a balanced calculation on material grounds, developed from a blandly unimpassioned 'why not?' But if all this is to suggest that loss of Parasha alone is an improbable cause of Evgenii's madness, his condition must presumably be related instead to the destruction of that dream of peaceful contentment and lasting (до грóба) stability of which Parasha was a part (a more egocentric, less sympathetic cause than selflessly devoted love – which returns us, perhaps at a new level of existential acuteness, to consideration of the intrinsic worth of family happiness). And given Evgenii's lukewarm enthusiasms, this should perhaps be related in turn to the sudden, horrified realisation that life is simply not comfortably well-ordered, harmonious and predictable. Unlike the created city with its стрóгий, стрóйный вид, the future cannot be mapped out with deliberate certainty; and man is helplessly vulnerable, with no safe refuge (дом, приют). Moreover, the shock of Parasha's untimely death perhaps reveals to Evgenii not just the fragility – or futility – of calculations of enduring happiness and security, but also an inherent unfairness in the unravelling of individual fate such as is already dimly implicit in his night-time ruminations on the fortunes of others, and is amplified at the end of Part 1 in the sentiment that life is the mockery of heaven at earth's expense. Who dies young or survives to enjoy their grandchildren, who is or is not born to 'brains and money' – or even creative genius – are matters which reflect an apparent arbitrariness, perhaps an emptiness (cf. сон пустóй) of sense, over which there is no individual control.

Whereas comparable perceptions of the injustice of being might prompt the strong Romantic hero – a character such as Pushkin's Salieri – to the powerful rhetoric and poisonous deeds of grand, satanic rebellion, it is striking that Evgenii instead founders in spineless capitulation. But then, of course, the climactic moment of his own rebellious gesture of defiance against the Bronze Horseman, the alleged author of *his* fate, introduces a new twist. Evgenii's second confrontation with the statue appears to signal a restitution of dignity and inner worth, intimated in part by lexical parallels suggesting his comparability with Peter (see ll. 403, 428 and notes) and even the elements (see below). The threat which he directs against Peter's 'haughty idol' (ll. 434-8) can readily be taken not just as a gesture of personal resentment, but as the symbolic protest of oppressed against oppressor, even of democrat against autocrat and tyrant (*inter alia*, the 'black force', сила чёрная, which grips Evgenii might conceivably bear connotations of чернь, the popular rabble). Many commentators have also detected an allusion to the Decembrist Revolt which took place on the same square the year after the flood, in 1825 – a line of interpretation apparently reinforced by the possibility of veiled references to Decembrism elsewhere in the text (see Notes.) If, moreover, Evgenii is indeed the product of the Petrine system, this perhaps means that social discontent and political rebellion are an inherent consequence of Peter's creation. This would point once more to the tsar's human fallibility at a point where Evgenii's stature reaches its zenith, and lend long-term, extra-personal menace to Evgenii's 'Just you wait' (Ужо́ тебе́!). It might also help to account for the extreme, seemingly disproportionate reaction by which the humble madman's outburst stirs the hitherto imperturbable, immovable statue into protracted, thunderous pursuit.

On a personal level, the 'terrifying clarification' of Evgenii's thoughts which initiates the scene of confrontation (ll. 404-5) implies a profound moment of dramatic insight into truth. It perhaps brings to mind the privileged perceptions of the holy fool of Orthodox tradition and *wanderprophet* of Romantic fashion. No less significantly in the light of what has been said above, it seems akin also to the penetrating illumination of creative inspiration. If Pushkin's earlier depiction of Peter echoed 'The Poet', so, now, does his depiction of Evgenii.* Like Evgenii (but not Peter, in this respect), the poet in that poem is possibly the most inconsequential (ничто́жный) of all men – until the sudden onset of inspiration transforms him completely. 'Wild and stern' (ди́кий и суро́вый; cf. Evgenii's ди́кие взо́ры, l. 426, and other occurrences of ди́кий throughout *The Bronze Horseman*), he then shuns the world and its amusements, flees the human crowd – and does not bow down his 'proud head' before earthly potentates, at 'the feet of the popular idol' (куми́р, another recurrent word in *The Bronze Horseman*). Evgenii, it might be inferred, undergoes a comparable experience of self-

---

*The descriptive parallels to Evgenii in 'The Poet' are also noted in the somewhat different interpretation of Catharine T. Nepomnyashchy, 'The Poet, History and the Supernatural: A Note on Pushkin's *The Bronze Horseman*', in A. Mandelker and R. Reeder (eds), *The Supernatural in Slavic and Baltic Literatures: Essays in Honor of Victor Terras* (Columbus, Ohio: Slavica, 1988), pp. 37-41 (34-46). For Evgenii's approximation to the figure of poet, compare also Pushkin's poem 'God grant I do not lose my mind' (Не дай мне Бог сойти с ума́, written in the same year as *The Bronze Horseman*), in which the creative inspiration of the Romantics is inherently a form of madness.

realisation and self-validation: a spiritual transformation which liberates morally and politically, as well as elevates and illuminates.

The inevitable counter-argument is twofold: not just that the moment passes all too quickly from seeming triumph into abject defeat, but that it perhaps never makes sense at all. Evgenii's immediate, horrified retreat from the implications of his deed (ll. 438 ff.), the persecution of his nocturnal pursuit, and the continuing, degrading contrition (ll. 456-64) which is part of his lingering decline through a-historical limbo into ignominious death (no sudden, tragic execution!), might together readily outweigh the considerations just outlined, to suggest that if rebellion is indeed a flaw in Peter's scheme, it is not a fatal one. Evgenii's spontaneous protest – and by implication that of the Decembrists, or of the Poles in 1830-1 (cf. the echoes of Mickiewicz described in the Notes) – is impotent and self-destructive folly: a futile gesture, crushed with a ruthlessness that brings little credit to either side. (There may also be a bitterly self-deprecatory allegory of Pushkin-Evgenii's own relation to the imperial authority of Peter-Nicholas, with which, in 1826, he had mistakenly considered himself an equal, only to experience subsequent persecution, and be cowed into humiliating submission: cf. Gutsche, pp. 41, 155.) Further interpretation hinges on our estimation of the quality of Evgenii's insight: whether, as rebel, he confronts the statue in an access of inspired lucidity or genuine, unrelieved insanity. Is all rebellion, unplanned or otherwise, therefore inherently insane? In marked contrast to the passage first introducing Evgenii, Pushkin now refrains from direct interiorisation. The most tangible evidence are therefore the words Evgenii utters; and these are so ill-expressed that they border on incoherence (see ll. 436-8 and notes). Though Evgenii may be sufficiently inspired to imagine the supernatural pursuit, words (and rationality) fail him; and thus, when he eventually emerges onto 'the shores of the empty waves', he cannot lend coherent form to his experience, but lapses into the terminal silence of an anonymous death. Evgenii earlier dreams 'like a poet' (l. 144), but in truth he is no more a poet than a Peter (perhaps, in his 'blackness', closer to the rabble whose imprecations the true poet can ignore with impunity: cf. 'The Poet and the Rabble'; Поэ́т и чернь); and the outward resemblances which the text discloses – if they do not actively mislead (as well they might) – otherwise remain just that. Devoid of inner substance, they emphasise the gulf between what Evgenii is and what he is not (and might or might nearly have become).

If Peter's function in the poem is primarily connected with multiplicity of meaning, Evgenii's, we might now conclude, is connected with its loss or absence, and failed restitution. After disaster has struck, he is so overwhelmed by its arbitrariness that he reacts at a crucial point with crazed laughter. Confronted with apparent absurdity, he becomes himself an absurd figure. (The term, associated with the literature of a later era, derives from the Latin *surdus*, 'deaf'; appropriately enough, Evgenii is 'deafened' by the noise of inner anxiety: ll. 374-5.)* He exists in a state of nervous dread, and so loses his grip on surroundings and self that he becomes unable to function within social norms, to communicate with others, or to use language constructively (talking to self, laughter, inarticulate threat, silence). Where Peter is engaged in construction, Evgenii, indeed, seems often engaged in inappropriate misconstruction. His misapprehensions begin when he maps out his comfortable future (and under-estimates the worsening weather). They continue through inappropriate expectation of protection from Peter (end Part 1?), over-reaction (!) to the aftermath of the flood, or perception of the immobile statue in headlong motion; and arguably persist to the very end, in uncertainty as to whether the 'empty' (chaos, the senseless void; cf. the 'empty dream' at the end of Part 1: l. 249), ruined (= unidentifiable?) hut is indeed that of Parasha (cf. ll. 472-4 and note). In all this, 'poor Evgenii' hovers uncertainly on the border between the pitiable and the pitiful, his notionally tragic humanity tainted by elements of black comedy which leave the issue of sympathy profoundly problematic.

The elements

Among Evgenii's misunderstandings, one of the most egregious may be identifying Peter as the cause of his woes. In the most literal sense, Evgenii's hopes were destroyed not by the tsar, but by a natural disaster, the flood (indeed, the very frenzy with which he turns against Peter may betoken the frustration of displaced aggression). To rail against wind and water is particularly senseless; it might also seem tantamount to questioning the whole of God's order (and there is an overtone of blasphemy in Evgenii's uttered threat: see l. 436 and note). From this point of view, Evgenii's alleged 'clarification of thought' is a manifest obfuscation.

Be that as it may, the 'natural elements' and their impact occupy a far larger part of Pushkin's text than the absent Peter and the invisible Parasha: nature, in this ostensibly urban poem, is at least as prominent as the city itself (cf. Briggs 1990, p. 177). Moreover, Pushkin's description of storm and flood involves his most imaginative imagery and inventive similes, his most vivid lexicon, and many of his most accomplished poetic effects. There is, of course, more to this than mere generation of narrative interest in the provision of a stirring backdrop to the main story (or stories) of Peter and Evgenii. Briggs, in particular, has argued eloquently that the forces of nature are, on the most profound level, the true centre of the poem, which shows man at the mercy of a natural environment over which his sovereignty is

---

*I am indebted to Professor Neil Cornwell for insights into the nature of the literary absurd.

pure illusion. As Pushkin's choice of language (particularly adjectives and verbs) powerfully implies, man is 'poor', puny and pitiable; nature, by contrast, is 'strong, enviable and admirable'. It may even exhibit not so much an awesome indifference, as some specifically anti-human delight in its destruction of man's endeavours, animated by 'a disgusting spirit of play, mockery and out-and-out enmity'. At any rate, the socio-political tensions encircling Peter and Evgenii, Russia's struggle for nationhood and the like, seem of relative insignificance on the cosmic scale of the impotence of all men, tsar and subject alike, before vaster forces: those elements which, despite the exhortation of the Introduction, are by no means vanquished (cf. побеждённая стихия, l. 87), and never will be so (Briggs, 1990, pp. 176-92).

Quite apart from the horrific devastation caused with such ease by the marauding flood – which retreats of its own accord, not because of anything man can do – this interpretation finds substantial support from two further episodes. One is the poem's ending, when Evgenii's sorry death in some natural void beyond the shelter of the city emphasises the 'ironic smallness and insignificance' of every human endeavour ('You dream, you act, you build, but it is all without meaning and value'). The other – 'the saddest moment in the poem' according to Briggs, 'if we can bring ourselves to think in broader terms about the true capabilities and limitations of men' – is the appearance of Alexander I on the palace balcony at the height of the flood:

Печа́лен, сму́тен, вы́шел он
И мо́лвил: «С Бо́жией стихи́ей
Царя́м не совладе́ть».

Even the tsars are rendered helpless (Briggs, 1983, pp. 133, 123). Yet it is by now scarcely surprising that the central elements of the interpretative argument may also contain the seeds of the counter-argument. In other words, it could be objected that it is Alexander, not Peter, who speaks these fateful words; and perhaps, after all, not all tsars are equal. Alexander's passive capitulation – symptomatic of an inertia satirised throughout the surrounding passage – surely aligns him with Evgenii, not Peter; whereas if ever anyone were able to 'master' – or 'co-rule with' – the elements, Peter, by contrast, surely did so. True, the flood inflicted serious damage, but primarily to primitive buildings and structures of 'pre-Petrine' wood. The Petrine core, the magnificent city of stone and its imperious bronze statue, survives impervious and intact: even if the waters are to encroach again, there is no reason to suppose it will not continue to endure, as permanent, at least, as the entirety of human culture. And though the ending indeed strikes a supra-historical, cosmic note (leading us, amongst other things, to wonder whether the elements of which Alexander spoke are 'God's' at all), it also, surely, points us back to the opening. The poem is not unambiguously linear, and we are led full circle from devastation to an act of construction which, it should be recalled, was performed in accord with nature (Приро́дой здесь нам сужде́нó...; l. 15). It might even be concluded that Peter's achievement was, precisely, to 'co-rule' on an equal footing with nature – the occasional, inevitable encroachments of which he accommodated into his scheme of things, in the same way as human suffering and rebellious discontent. (The river, with its stately current, is after all an essential part of his design, and the fullness of his thought 'rhymes' with the waves from the very outset.) In so doing, he becomes like nature himself: a vast, impassive, mythical, superhuman force, defiance of which, as Evgenii confirms, is truly insensate: as meaningless as a challenge to nature.

It should be emphasised that this is not to reject Briggs' view of the meanings attaching to nature. Like the hints of Apocalypse, the sense of nature's dwarfing presence, once intimated, is never entirely dispelled; indeed, it would be foolish to deny that it is an important and thought-provoking aspect of the poem's total meaning. The difficulty is simply in abstracting a single thematic stand (mighty elements – puny man), unqualified, as over-arching message. For whereas Briggs maintains that 'Either the poem suggests final victory for Peter (or man) over the elements or it does not; it is not possible to argue both ways' (1990, p. 179), the thrust of the preceding paragraphs, as of this Introduction as a whole, is that, for Pushkin at least, this is entirely possible. Peter, in this case, can both fulfil his destiny in working with nature (l. 15), and stand against it. It is the very essence of *The Bronze Horseman* that Pushkin habitually 'argues both ways', simultaneously entertaining competing, even apparently mutually exclusive attitudes.

Conclusion

A different approach to the problem of 'what the poem is about', to which the discussion now returns, is suggested by the work of the pre-eminent scholar Iu.M. Lotman. Pushkin, in many of his writings, deals with the conflict between two concepts or entities (freedom – civilisation, Mozart – Salieri, etc.). *The Bronze Horseman*, however, might better be described by the more complex model of tripartite, rather than bipartite opposition. In other words, to simplify and liberally adapt the categories of Lotman's more sophisticated analysis,* we might think of the multiple meanings Pushkin generates in terms of an equilateral triangle (XYZ), the nodes of which correspond (in no order of precedence) to Evgenii, Peter, and 'the

---

*Yuri M. Lotman, *Universe of the Mind: A Semiotic Theory of Culture*, trans. Ann Shukman (London: I.B. Tauris, 1990), pp. 82-6.

elements'. Each of these 'nodes' is persistently (re-)combined with and (re-) opposed to each of the others. Thus Peter (Y) is challenged and opposed by both Evgenii and the elements (X-Z), and sets himself against both in turn. Yet Peter is also *likened* to the elements (Y-Z) – in part, in opposition to Evgenii (X), who is their common victim; and there is a commonality too between Peter and Evgenii in their opposition to the natural forces of storm and flood. (Diagrammatically: Y ↔ X-Z; X ↔ Y-Z; Z ↔ Y-X). We might refine this hypothetical triangle – perhaps, as it were, extending it onto another plane or dimension, to take account of the supernatural and religious-metaphysical speculations – but we should not subtract from it, to take any one of its sides (or nodes) as the true axis of meaning, outweighing the importance of the others: the poem is simultaneously 'about' all the relation-ships the design encompasses. The sides of the triangle, moreover, should perhaps be regarded as an endless (and endlessly reversible) continuum, which precludes the interruption of a linear resolution; and it is a less conven-tional property of this hypothetical figure that the 'identity' of each of its nodes is remarkably fluid: potentially so broad and mutable as to embrace logical incompatibilities, in a thorough contingency upon the content of each of the other nodes, and the particular directionality of the axes. Put another way, 'Peter' as antithesis to the flood is, for example, different to 'Peter' as antithesis to Evgenii. In different 'contexts' he might embody reason and enlightenment, or irrationality and darkness; the impersonal historical force pitted against the rights of the individual, or the individual creator, pitted against the chaotic void of the scattered elements. Evgenii is alternately rebellious and submissive; he invites pity and contempt. The river is tamed and the river is uncontrollable. And so one could continue.

If it might be hoped that this notional construct helps to explain why it is difficult to define what the poem is about, it might also, finally, go some way toward accounting for the exceptional density of its verbal structure. Part of the poem's complexity comes from Pushkin's perennial fondness for 'situational rhyme', for repeating a situation, generally with extensive verbal echoes, in a fresh context which necessitates contrast, comparison and reinterpretation. The most obvious example are the two encounters between Evgenii and the statue. But in *The Bronze Horseman* it is perhaps more important that the contents of each of our triangular nodes are repeatedly contaminated by semantic fields belonging to the others. This might finally be illustrated by three simple examples.

The Introduction makes reference to the stately or 'sovereign' flow of the Neva: Невы́ держа́вное тече́нье. Clearly, the adjective places the river in the province of Peter's control (cf. also note to ll. 81-3). Yet it may also suggest the river's own sovereign power, ultimately subject to no human 'conquest' (l. 87). Part 1 opens as follows:

Над омрачённым Петроградом
Дышал ноябрь осенним хладом.

The verb is vaguely anthropomorphic, again encouraging us to read the elements in terms of the human. Conversely, the human may also be read in terms of the elemental ambience, by which it seems infected. *Mrachnost'* will later be a quality of Evgenii (l. 432); equally, though, *mrak* will also signify the province governed by the not-exactly-human bronze idol (l. 411). Naturally, the complexity already apparent in this single lexical strand is vastly increased over larger segments of text. The waters and the flood, for instance, are characterised by such adjectives as возмущённый (l. 257), наглый (l. 261) or мятёжный (l. 351) which link both with Evgenii and rebellion, to imply that his protest is not a lone one, but part of an elemental tide; and that the elements themselves may stand for human political rebellion. They are also described, however, as full of 'victorious triumph' (l. 279) and like the breathing of a horse returned from battle (ll. 283-4). This seems instead to prompt association with Peter, his statue, and his military prowess. Perhaps the 'rebellious' flood is simultaneously a destructive agent of the tsar's will? Verbal echoes, drawing parallels between one image or concept and another, create the impression that each component is viewed and reviewed stereoscopically, from many angles; and these echoes really do seem to extend almost indefinitely, lending the poem its endless richness.

We might conclude, therefore, that like his depiction of Peter, Pushkin's poem as a whole is deeply concerned with the generation and 'meaning' of meaning. Yet when untenably simplistic, linear solutions are discarded, there is often a remarkably fine line between complex multiplicity of meaning, and its absence or degeneration into inarticulacy: between, that is, *polnota* and *pustota*, (Peter's) construction and (Evgenii's) misconstruction. Nor is it entirely clear where meaning originates. It may be God-given and omnipresent, for man to unravel. It may be instead that, without human input, existence is fundamentally devoid of meaning. If so, its production is a matter of inner resource: one might succumb to the silence of non-being, or, like tsar, or poet – the tsar-poet whose private being nevertheless in some ways closely converged with 'poor Evgenii's' – triumphantly create enduring structure and sense.

Ultimately, though, uncertainty follows uncertainty and creative triumph alike. Does Pushkin's eulogy of St Petersburg, for instance, indeed possess real substance; or is it, in the final analysis, no more than hollow rhetoric, a dazzling shell of empty words? It remains for the reader to judge.

THE PETERSBURG BACKGROUND

History

Tradition has it that St Petersburg was founded on Trinity Day, 16 May 1703. Legends variously link its foundation – by Peter I himself, who supposedly cut two strips of turf and laid them in the form of a cross, declaring 'A city shall be here!' (Здесь быть гóроду; cf. Pushkin, l. 13) – with the relics of St Andrew the Apostle (who 'brought Christianity to Russia') or, in some versions, of the Russian warrior-prince St Alexander Nevskii; and with an eagle which hallowed Peter's enterprise, like the eagle which led the first Christian Emperor, Constantine, to the site of Constantinople-Byzantium.

More realistically, as Pushkin suggests (l. 12), the city's origins relate to Peter's conduct of the Great Northern War against Sweden (1700-21) – then Russia's most powerful neighbour and the greatest power in Northern Europe. Sweden, which occupied territories ceded by Russia in the Livonian Wars of the 16th and 17th centuries, inflicted a crushing defeat at Narva in 1700, prompting Peter to radical reform of the Russian army. After some minor successes in the Baltic, the Russians rallied to capture the Swedish fortress of Nöteburg on Lake Ladoga, at the source of the Neva, in October 1702 (Peter promptly renamed it Schlüsselberg, the 'key' to the Neva and the Baltic); and the fortress and town of Nienschants at the confluence of the Okhta and the Neva on 1 May 1703. Instead of reinforcing Nienschants, Peter used looted materials and Swedish prisoners to build a new fortress in a more strategically advantageous location, on the small Zaiachii or Hare's Island (some 600 × 350 metres) a mile or so closer to the mouth of the Neva. The hexagonal-shaped fortress, hurriedly constructed in a spot by no means as uninhabited as the patriotic mythologisation of Pushkin's Introduction would suggest (Nienschants was large enough to boast several sawmills and trade-links with Lübeck and Amsterdam, and there were some forty villages and smaller settlements in the immediate vicinity!), was named after the church within its walls, dedicated on 29 June, the feast-day of Saints Peter and Paul. The city which grew up around it was also named (at first in the Dutch manner, as Sankt-Piter-burkh) not, as is often supposed, in honour of the tsar, but after his patron saint, St Peter the Apostle.

A Swedish naval withdrawal in October 1703 allowed Peter to establish an artillery battery and fortress (the future Kronshtadt) on Kotlin Island at the very mouth of the Neva, and with this protection, to develop outward from the St Peter and Paul site. Dwelling places and a wooden Trinity Cathedral were constructed on the adjacent island (modern Petrovskii Island), as well as the beginnings of the commercial port (a Dutch merchant ship put in to the Fortress as early as November 1703) which was shortly transferred to Vasil'evskii Island. A fortified shipyard, the Admiralty, was founded slightly downstream, on the left bank of the Neva. Though the military and commercial aspects celebrated in Pushkin's Introduction were thus prominent from the outset, Peter nevertheless wanted more than a mere port with a 'firm footing' on the Baltic. He had plans for a capital on the model of Western European cities he had visited, and even, as he put it as early as 1706, a 'paradise'. (He had already found time to concern himself with the delivery of peonies and fragrant blooms, and soon drafted in an expert on fountains: his 'Summer Garden' was the innovatory precursor of the many formal gardens and parks admired by Pushkin [ll. 37-8], which the city's richest inhabitants would subsequently concentrate on the more suitable of the many lesser islands in the Neva delta.) A major victory over the Swedes at Poltava in 1709 and the capture of Baltic fortresses including those of Vyborg and Riga in 1710 enabled further building to proceed in increased security. 1710 saw the inception of work on the first major non-military projects, including the Summer and Winter Palaces (the latter the first of three), the stone palaces of Peter's favourite, A.D. Menshikov, and other dignitaries, the Alexander Nevskii Monastery, and so on. St Petersburg became the Russian capital in 1712 or 1713 (there is no formal record), with the effective transfer from Moscow of, respectively, the tsar's court and the Senate.

Building continued at a pace ruthlessly enforced by Peter, and at his death, in 1725, the city had over 6,000 dwellings and a permanent population of 40,000 (or perhaps as many as 90,000 including troops and temporary conscript workers, of whom more below). Yet not everything proceeded according to the smooth plan which Pushkin and other apologists of Peter might suggest. The first urban development, to the east of the Trinity Cathedral, was so haphazard that it was decided to begin the centre anew on Vasil'evskii Island, following a strict geometric grid of avenues and canals. Practical obstacles also forced the abandonment of this second endeavour to create a Westernised (Amsterdamian?) world of regularity and order, and development eventually shifted to the left bank. The Больша́я першпекти́вная доро́га (*pershpektiva* – prospect, a wide and straight avenue – from the Latin *prospecto*, to look into the distance: cf. Pushkin's l.3), renamed Nevskii Prospekt, was begun in 1715, but the upper part, further from the Admiralty, continually foundered in marshy ground and had to be re-laid in the 1730s. And so on. Inevitably, too, much of the construction under Peter reflected practical rather than aesthetic priorities, with the provision of a foundry and arsenal, artillery works and powder factories, rope- and brickworks, leather and cloth works, sawmills, breweries, and the like.

In essence, Petersburg acquired the magnificent contours praised by Pushkin during the hundred years (l. 21) or so after Peter's death. Relatively neglected by his immediate successors, its development flourished under his daughter Elizabeth (reigned 1741-62) – whose favourite Rastrelli's contributions included the third, still extant Winter Palace and the Smol'nyi Convent – and under Catherine the Great (reigned 1762-96), who encouraged a more restrained classicism. The granite facing of the Neva, twice mentioned in Pushkin's poem (ll. 35, 46), was carried out in the central part of Petersburg only in 1763-88. Other famous landmarks of the still 'youthful' city (l. 21) arose during Pushkin's own lifetime, particularly in a spate of building following the Russian victory over Napoleon. In addition to the 'new' Admiralty, reconstructed in 1806-23 (see l. 54 and note), Kazan' Cathedral, for example, was finished in 1811, the Stock Exchange on the spit of Vasil'evskii Island (where 'ships from all the ends of the earth' still docked) in 1810 and the adjoining Customs Houses in 1829-33. The enormous General Staff building rounded off the 'circle' of Palace Square in 1829. At the time Pushkin was writing *The Bronze Horseman*, new Senate and Synod buildings (1829-34) were nearing completion on Senate Square, site of Peter's statue and still at that time a huge open (or empty!) space, unencumbered by later gardens. Work was also in progress behind, on the monumental project for St Isaac's Cathedral, the huge external columns for which had been erected in 1828-30. The Cathedral was eventually completed only in 1858. Pushkin in 1833, in other words, must still have had a vivid sense of the city's newness, whilst also realising that the construction work initiated by Peter was finally reaching its triumphant conclusion.

There was also of course a dark underside to St Petersburg's constructive splendour. In some ways, it merely deceived. Peter's first wooden cottage of 1703 was painted in red segments so as to resemble brick. The first wooden Peter and Paul church was likewise painted to look like stone and yellow marble, and Peter was soon to decree the use of a construction method using clay over wooden frames (*mazanki*), to give the entire city the false appearance of being made of stone. Later, of course, the more opulent buildings tended to line the waterfronts, masking squalor behind. Somewhat more grimly, nobles and merchants as well as humble artisans were forced in their thousands to populate the 'Northern capital', and obliged to comply with Peter's incessant, often onerous and contradictory decrees concerning building and maintenance. More unfortunate were the far larger numbers drafted in to build the city. Though targets were generally not met, by 1707 Peter was intending to conscript a work force of 40,000 per year, taken from selected regions near and far, and supplemented by prisoners of war, criminals and beggars. Climate, sickness, under-nourishment, and unremitting labour with inadequate equipment resulted quite literally in countless deaths (Peter did not concern to keep statistics on the subject). His city was built, as the historian Karamzin would put it, on 'tears and corpses', and it became a huge cemetery for the people. Many of the contrasts and ambiguities which underlie Pushkin's poem were incorporated from the outset into the very fabric of the city it describes.

Flood and disaster

Though there is no doubt that an outlet on the Baltic was of immense strategic importance to Peter and Russia, the particular site which he persisted in developing, even when he might have moved on, had several inherent disadvantages. The inconvenience of its island structure (there are over 100 islands, large and small, within the present-day city) may have appealed to a tsar who had been obsessed with boats since childhood; but he and his successors also had to contend with an inhospitable climate, marshy terrain (though much of the land had previously been cultivated) and the ravages of a persistent vulnerability to flood. The latter is not simply the result of relatively low-lying terrain. The particular location and configuration of the wide mouth of the Neva, at the eastern end of the Finnish Gulf, are such that a combination of persistent strong wind from the west or south-west, and the suction effect of cyclonic pressure, are capable of stemming and forcing back upon themselves many of the smaller river outlets which criss-cross the area, and even on occasion the main course of the Neva. A large volume of water from the Gulf is pushed upstream, amid massive turbulence, and where the powerful surge breaks against water flowing downstream, the many river-channels and canals are liable to burst their relatively low banks. Given the way such flooding is caused, however, the water will also subside and flow outward again relatively quickly.

In the early years of the city's existence, floods were an almost annual occurrence. The first was in August 1703. A second was recorded in 1706 when Peter, whose own apartments were temporarily awash to a height of 21 inches, managed to find cause for merriment: 'It was very amusing to see people sitting on roofs and trees – not only men, but women too', he wrote to Menshikov. 'Although the water was very great, it did not do much damage.' In 1720, on the other hand, he put to death one of the earliest of the many prophets of doom who warned of God's wrath against the tsar, and publicly foretold the city's destruction by flood that September.

The gradual construction of embankments subsequently somewhat reduced the frequency of flooding, as did the construction of one or two canals specially calculated to combat the problem (e.g. the Ekaterininskii and Obvodnyi, completed respectively in 1790 and 1834). Building and canal-excavation work, and even the accumulation of refuse, contributed to a quite significant raising of land levels, which assisted in many areas. Disasters nevertheless continued to occur. A flood of 1729 was sufficiently calamitous to prompt Peter II to consider abandoning the city altogether. There were comparable or worse incursions in 1744, 1752, 1755, and so on; while the worst flood of the 18th century, with the waters rising by over 10 feet, was in 1777. There were many casualties and huge financial losses. None, however, was so severe as the flood of November 1824, described in Pushkin's poem, when the waters rose by more than 13 feet.

Rather like Peter before him, Pushkin reacted to news of the flood, when it first reached him in Mikhailovskoe, with ribald humour ('Voilà une belle occasion à vos dames de faire bidet', he wrote to his brother, joking also about Noah and the disgorged contents of the city's wine-cellars). According to the possibly conservative estimate of S. Aller, however, the flood took 480 lives, and swept away 462 homes and buildings. Many more were damaged. More than 3500 cattle were lost, together with many commercial goods and private possessions, while damage to infrastructure (bridges and the like) and trade amounted to tens of millions of roubles. As Pushkin became aware of the scale of the disaster, the initial amusement which is arguably reflected in some elements of his poem naturally gave way to compassion for the victims, and irritation at the government's ineffectual measures of restitution. 'I cannot stop thinking about this flood, which is not at all as funny as first seems', he now wrote to his brother (4 December 1824), and suggested that he use the money due from the first chapter of *Onegin* to make an anonymous donation to some unfortunate victim. It might also be noted, however, that Pushkin's approval of a decision to suspend theatrical performances as a mark of respect was tinged with political anxiety ('...the people [народ] should not be irritated by offensive opulence. Shopkeepers seeing the lights in the dress circle might break the mirrored windows, and losses would ensue'). It is perhaps significant to the future poem's symbolism that a connection between flood and popular rebellion was already implicitly made.

With the possible causes of Evgenii's madness in mind, it should be added that life in St Petersburg was precarious in other ways too. Fire was a constant threat, particularly in the poorer, wooden quarters where it claimed many lives. So was disease, often in conjunction with the unhealthy climate: respiratory diseases such as pneumonia and tuberculosis were a frequent cause of premature death, as of course were conditions resulting from exposure to the cold. A slightly different phenomenon was the cholera epidemic of 1831, which by mid-June was claiming 600 lives a day (more than the flood of 1824!), and led the government to decree that burials should be conducted only by night. Popular resentment at this and other ineffectual measures caused widespread unrest, and on 22 June there was a riot before a temporary hospital on Sennaia Square. Nicholas I, who had earlier departed for the more sanitary conditions of Peterhof on the Finnish Gulf, hurriedly returned and, with considerable courage, quelled the discontent by addressing the rioters in person from an open carriage. The incident may suggest another interpretative possibility for Pushkin's image of elemental-popular rebellion, truly directed more against human mortality than political iniquity, majestically countered by the decisive action of a previously remote autocrat.

In all, life-expectancy in Petersburg was lower than elsewhere in Russia and, most unusually for the 19th century, deaths constantly and significantly outnumbered births. Petersburgers were often regarded as hypochondriacs and melancholics, and the incidence of mental illness, alcoholism and suicide was dramatically higher than in other cities. And as if the natural forces that inflicted the inhabitants of 'Peter's creation' were not enough, another man-made source of misery was demographic. Quite apart from the fact that most lived in cramped and inadequate accommodation, in the year of Pushkin's death the city's population was 70% male and only 30% female. Inevitably, for many poor clerks the dream of wife and home remained hopelessly unobtainable.

Peter's statue

The equestrian statue of Peter the Great, known from Pushkin's poem as 'The Bronze Horseman' and itself a quintessential symbol of St Petersburg, was unveiled to much pomp, popular celebration and military ceremony on 7 August 1782, the official centenary of Peter's accession to the throne. In an elaborate piece of theatre which was played out before the Empress Catherine, gigantic painted screens, previously erected to conceal the monument, fell away at a signal volley of artillery 'to reveal to the astonished eyes of the spectators' – in the words of a contemporary document – 'Peter on his steed, seeming to ride out from the bowels of the [screen-painted] mountain, onto a huge rock, with outstretched, imperious arm'. There followed a march-past of no less than 15,000 troops, multiple salutes of cannon, rifle and drum, and elaborate 'illuminations'.

There may have been an element of relief in all this, for the statue – 5.3 metres high, on a stone pedestal rising to over 8 metres from the ground – had been fourteen years in preparation. It had first been commissioned by a younger and less secure Catherine, seeking in the early years of a reign initiated by the murder of Peter the Great's legitimate grandson, her husband Peter III, to establish her own legitimate connection to her illustrious predecessor. The laconic inscription in both Russian and Latin which eventually appeared on the statue's plinth (Петру́ Первому Екатери́на Втора́я: PETRO primo CATHARINA secunda) signalled this with forceful dignity. Catherine is 'second' in direct relation only to Peter – not, however, to his wife, Catherine I, or any other intermediary.

Catherine's symbolic tribute was ordered after she had rejected a project to furnish the pedestal for an already extant statue of Peter – the first equestrian statue in Russia, cast in 1740 to a model made by the elder Rastrelli in the 1720s. (This now stands outside the Engineers' Castle, where it was placed by Catherine's son Paul I in a deliberate affront to his mother's memory.) Largely on the recommendation of her illustrious correspondent, the French *philosophe* Diderot, Catherine then turned to the sculptor Etienne Maurice Falconet (1716-91), who duly arrived in Russia in 1766. His naturally slow and meticulous work on a project which might conceivably have been completed for the centenary of Peter's *birth* in 1772 was continually impeded by bureaucratic wrangles and practical setbacks.

There was protracted argument even over the general conception of the statue. Court dignitaries led by the official administrator of the project, Count Betskii, favoured a portrayal of imperial authority in the manner of the famous bronze statue of Marcus Aurelius on the Capitoline in Rome: with right arm extended in triumph, the Roman Emperor rides his powerful horse forward at a stately walk across the level surface of a flat pedestal. Falconet, however, maintained that Peter's distinctive essence could be captured only by a more dramatic dynamism of forward (and upward) movement. He sought also to dispense with the conventional embellishment of multiple allegorical figures, counselled by Diderot and much favoured in the 18th century. 'My monument will be simple', he retorted. 'I will limit myself simply to a statue of this hero, whom I treat neither as a great general nor as a conqueror, though of course he was both those things. Much higher is the personality of the creator, the law-giver, the benefactor of his country, and this is what people must be shown. My tsar does not hold a sceptre, he stretches his beneficent arm over the country throughout which he journeys. He climbs to the summit of the cliff which serves as his pedestal: this is an emblem of the difficulties he has overcome....' Peter's robes also caused dispute. Though crowned with laurels, Falconet chose to depict his rider not in the Roman garb of victor, but in a loose cape and simple attire (and also with an animal skin instead of a saddle), combining, to the irritation of Catherine's court, the identifiably Roman and the traditionally Russian. 'Peter's dress', he insisted, 'is the clothing of all nations, all peoples, all times, in a word, a hero's costume'.*

The more practical search for a suitable stone for the statue's base lasted for over a year, and was successfully concluded only through public appeal. It took two years more and well over a thousand workers to transport by land and sea from Karelia, a mere twelve miles away, the 'wild rock', the so-called thunder-stone (Гром-ка́мень), weighing almost 2000 tonnes in unworked form, which was eventually selected. Disagreement over the siting of the statue – where precisely on the appropriately symbolic Square, facing the Neva, between Peter's creations of Admiralty and Senate? – dragged on for four years. Falconet's designs for the horseman's head were repeatedly rejected by Catherine, and a model prepared by his young assistant Marie-Anne Collot was accepted instead. The subsequent process of casting the bronze (which, through bitter experience of native ineptitude,

* Falconet's correspondence with Diderot is cited after Iu. Rakov, *Vokrug Mednogo vsadnika: V granite i stikhakh* (St Petersburg: Khimizdat, 1999), pp. 32, 34.

Falconet concluded he must organise personally) went wrong, causing a fire and injuring the sculptor and his Russian assistant. Part of the statue, from the horseman's knee upwards, had to be recast and joined to the rest two years later (1775, 1777). Not surprisingly, after further disagreement with Catherine and the continual jealous antagonism of Betskii, Falconet departed in exasperation in 1778, leaving Iu.M. Felten and F.G. Gordeev to complete his work. He did not return to Russia for the grand unveiling in 1782.

There is no need to expatiate here on the latent ambiguities of Falconet's dynamic creation (threatening or protecting, staring into the distance or squinting angrily at the viewer, etc.), which are consummately amplified in Pushkin's poem in ways already outlined in the Introduction. Nor is there any need to dwell on such matters as the allegorical implications (envy, treason, evil enemy, devil?) of the serpent which the horse tramples under-foot (in practical terms, a necessary third point of support for the rearing statue), which have no obvious relevance to Pushkin's text. It is perhaps worth noting, however, that popular imagination had preceded Pushkin in endowing the statue with supernatural vitality. One anecdote, recounted by various sources and sometimes related to the genesis of *The Bronze Horseman*, concerns the recurrent dream of one Major Baturin in 1812, when the imminent threat from Napoleon prompted Alexander I to consider remov-ing Peter's statue to safety elsewhere. Baturin imagined himself on Senate Square, where he saw Peter's statue turn its face, then descend from its plinth to gallop through the streets toward Alexander's palace. Impelled by some miraculous force Baturin followed, to hear the statue addressing Alexander with the promise: 'As long as I remain in place, my city has nothing to fear!' With that the horseman – here unequivocally the city's talismanic protector – turned back, and its 'sonorous and heavy gallop' resounded once more through the streets. Clearly, however, private conversations and contemplation of the possible meanings of Falconet's statue must have been at least as important as public anecdote in preparing the ground for Pushkin's poetic response. Against the famous lines:

> Не так ли ты над сáмой бéздной,
> На высотé, уздóй желéзной
> Россúю пóднял на дыбы́?

his old friend Prince Viazemskii later noted in his copy of *The Bronze Horseman*: 'My expression, uttered to Pushkin and Mickiewicz as we were walking past the statue'.

Literary refractions

By Pushkin's day, both Petersburg as a whole and such landmarks as Falconet's statue were already part of a well-established literary tradition.

His predecessors in writing of the city included such major poets as Lomonosov, Sumarokov, Derzhavin and Viazemeskii, and many lesser ones, among them Nikolev, Petrov, Bobrov, Shevyrev, Merzliakov, Kukol'nik, Ruban, Gnedich and Ryleev. As noted in the Introduction (p. viii), Pushkin's poem contains multiple echoes and some direct borrowings from this already sizeable body of Petersburg verse, which is predominantly odic-eulogistic in character. It even appears to draw on foreign prose accounts, such as Joseph de Maistre's *Soireés de Saint-Petersbourg*. By and large, however, even though aligning *The Bronze Horseman* to a tradition, and thereby also underscoring its departures therefrom, identification of Pushkin's many sources does not significantly aid interpretation of his poem's meaning. This can be illustrated by the following extract from Konstantin Batiushkov's prose work of 1814, 'A Stroll in the Academy of Sciences' (Прогу́лка в Акаде́мию Худо́жеств):

...looking at the Neva, covered in shipping, looking at the magnificent embankment upon which, due to habit, Petersburg's inhabitants look coldly, – admiring the countless people bustling beneath my window, this marvellous mingling of all nations, in which I could distinguish English and Asians, Frenchmen and Kalmyks, Russians and Finns, I asked myself the following question: what was here before Petersburg was built? Perhaps a pine wood, a damp, dreamy forest or a soft marsh (то́пкое боло́то), overgrown with moss and whortleberry; closer to the shore – a fisherman's hovel, around which were spread his various nets (мре́жи, невода́) and all the coarse tackle of his meagre trade... Here all was silent. Rarely did human voice break the stillness of this wild and gloomy wasteland (пустыня́ ди́кая, мра́чная), but now?

...And I imagined Peter, surveying for the first time the shores of the wild Neva, now so fine. The Swedish cannon were still roaring in the fortress of Nienschants; the mouth of the Neva was still controlled by the enemy, and frequent rifle shots were being fired along the marshy shores as the great idea took shape in the mind of the great man. Here will be a town (Здесь бу́дет го́род) he said, a miracle of light....Here Painting and the Arts, civil structures and laws will overcome nature itself. He spoke – and Petersburg arose from the wild swamp.

Readers of Pushkin's Introduction can have little doubt that it owes a substantial debt to this passage – although it is notably devoid of Pushkin's ambivalence. Its recognition may reveal something of Pushkin's characteristic artistic methods, but ultimately it does not diminish the originality of his more complex adaptation and it barely alters our understanding of his work.

This is not to deny, of course, that some of Pushkin's intertextual echoes were more obviously purposeful than others (see, for example, the reference to Viazemskii in the Notes, p. 50); and an exception must finally be made for the cycle of poems, bitterly satirical of St Petersburg, its symbolic equestrian statue, and its craven Russian inhabitants, which compose the *Digression* to Part 3 of the Polish poet Adam Mickiewicz's epic, *Forefathers' Eve*. This newly completed cycle was banned from publication in Russia; but Pushkin had a foreign edition with him when he left for the Urals and Boldino in 1833, and there is a sense in which the entirety of *The Bronze Horseman* is a rejoinder to Mickiewicz's invective. Some of the more conspicuous correspondences are therefore signalled in the Notes; more general discussion is offered in studies by Lednicki and Shvartsband. Ultimately, though, it might be argued that even here Pushkin's almost obsessive allusions to another text are part of a troubled private reflection on his own shifting position, which was vastly more ambivalent, both politically and artistically. In other words, what is finally at stake here, too, are the elusiveness and inconsistency which are fundamental to the success of his masterpiece.

BIBLIOGRAPHY

The best and most authoritative of the many Russian editions of *The Bronze Horseman* is in the prestigious 'Literaturnye pamiatniki' series: A.S. Pushkin, *Mednyi vsadnik*, ed. N.V. Izmailov (Leningrad: Nauka, 1978). In addition to a comprehensive publication of textual variants and a broad range of contemporary documents and literary sources, this contains a long essay by Izmailov on the history of the poem's conception and composition. With slight adjustments in capitalisation (see Note on Vocabulary, Style and Text, p. 53), it has been used as the source for the present text.

The suggestions given here for secondary reading represent a limited selection of what has seemed most useful or stimulating amid the voluminous critical literature on *The Bronze Horseman*, with some bias toward relatively accessible English-language materials. A much fuller Bibliography is to be found in Andrew Kahn's excellent monograph, which should also be consulted for a succinct overview of critical opinions and approaches to Pushkin's poem.

Selected Further Reading

Bayley, John, *Pushkin: A Comparative Commentary* (Cambridge: CUP, 1971).

Bethea, David, 'The Role of the *Eques* in Pushkin's *Bronze Horseman*', in D. Bethea (ed.), *Pushkin Today* (Bloomington and Indianapolis: Indiana U.P., 1993), pp. 99-118.

Briggs, A.D.P., *Alexander Pushkin: A Critical Study* (London and Canberra: Croom Helm,1983; repr. Bristol: The Bristol Press, 1991).

———*A Comparative Study of Pushkin's* The Bronze Horseman, *Nekrasov's* Red-Nosed Frost, *and Blok's* The Twelve: *The Wild World* (Lewiston and Lampeter: Edward Mellen, 1990).

Briusov, Va.Ia, '*Mednyi Vsadnik*', in his *Sobranie sochinenii*, 7 vols (Moscow: Khudozhestvennaia literatura, 1973-5), vol. 7, pp. 30-60.

Gasparov, B.M., *Poeticheskii iazyk Pushkina kak fakt istorii russkogo literaturnogo iazyka* (Vienna: Wiener Slawistischer Almanach, 1992).

Gregg, Richard, 'The Nature of Nature and the Nature of Eugene in *The Bronze Horseman*', *Slavic and East European Journal*, 21 (1977), pp. 167-79.

Gutsche, George J., 'Pushkin's *The Bronze Horseman*' in his *Moral Apostasy in Russian Literature* (Dekalb, Illinois: Northern Illinois U.P., 1986), pp. 16-42.

Hellie, Lillian J., 'The City as Myth and Symbol in Alexander Pushkin's Poem *The Bronze Horseman*', *Scando-Slavica*, 41 (1995), pp. 22-40.

Jakobson, Roman, *Pushkin and his Sculptural Myth* (The Hague: Mouton, 1975).

Kahn, Andrew, *Pushkin's* The Bronze Horseman (London: Bristol Classical Press, 1998).

Lednicki, W., *Pushkin's* Bronze Horseman: *The Story of a Masterpiece. With an Appendix including, in English, Mickiewicz's* Digression, *Pushkin's* Bronze Horseman, *and Other Poems* (1955; repr. Westport, Connecticut: Greenwood Press, 1978).

Ospovat A.L. and Timenchik R.D., *'Pechal'nu povest' sokhranit'...': Ob avtore i chitateliakh* Mednogo vsadnika (Moscow: Kniga, 1985).

Shvartsband, S., *Logika khudozhestvennogo poiska A.S. Pushkina ot Ezerskogo do* Pikovoi damy (Jerusalem: The Magnes Press, 1988).

Zekulin, Gleb, 'On Rereading *The Bronze Horseman*', *Canadian Slavonic Papers*, 29 (1987), pp. 228-40.

For reliable introductions to Russian versification, see Barry P. Scherr, *Russian Poetry: Meter, Rhythm, Rhyme* (Berkeley: California U.P., 1989); and to Peter the Great, see Lindsey Hughes, *Russia in the Age of Peter the Great* (New Haven and London: Yale U.P., 1998).

МÉДНЫЙ ВСÁДНИК

ПЕТЕРБÝРГСКАЯ ПÓВЕСТЬ

1833

ПРЕДИСЛÓВИЕ

Происшéствие, опи́санное в сей пóвести, оснóвано на и́стине. Подрóбности наводнéния заи́мствованы из тогдáшних журнáлов. Любопы́тные мóгут спрáвиться с извéстием, состáвленным *В. Н. Бéрхом.*

ВСТУПЛЕНИЕ

На берегу́ пусты́нных волн
Стоя́л Он, дум вели́ких полн,
И вдаль гляде́л. Пред ним широ́ко
Река́ несла́ся; бе́дный чёлн
По ней стреми́лся одино́ко.
По мши́стым, то́пким берега́м
Черне́ли и́збы здесь и там,
Приют убо́гого чухо́нца;
И лес, неве́домый луча́м
В тума́не спря́танного со́лнца
Круго́м шуме́л.

  И ду́мал Он:
Отсе́ль грози́ть мы бу́дем шве́ду.
Здесь бу́дет го́род заложён
На зло надме́нному сосе́ду.
Приро́дой здесь нам сужде́но
В Евро́пу проруби́ть окно́,[1]
Ного́ю твёрдой стать при мо́ре.
Сюда́ по но́вым им волна́м
Все фла́ги в го́сти бу́дут к нам
И запиру́ем на просто́ре.

  Прошло́ сто лет, и ю́ный град,
Полно́щных стран краса́ и ди́во,
Из тьмы лесо́в, из то́пи блат
Вознёсся пы́шно, горделиво;
Где пре́жде фи́нский рыболо́в,
Печа́льный па́сынок приро́ды,
Оди́н у ни́зких берего́в
Броса́л в неве́домые во́ды
Свой ве́тхий не́вод, ны́не там
По оживлённым берега́м
Грома́ды стро́йные тесня́тся
Дворцо́в и ба́шен; корабли́
Толпо́й со всех концо́в земли́
К бога́тым при́станям стремя́тся;

10

20

30

В грани́т оде́лася Нева́;
Мосты́ пови́сли над вода́ми;
Темно-зелёными сада́ми
Её покры́лись острова́,
И перед мла́дшею столи́цей
40 Поме́ркла ста́рая Москва́,
Как перед но́вою цари́цей
Порфироно́сная вдова́.

Люблю́ тебя́, Петра́ творе́нье,
Люблю́ твой стро́гий, стро́йный вид,
Невы́ держа́вное тече́нье,
Берегово́й её грани́т,
Твои́х огра́д узо́р чугу́нный,
Твои́х заду́мчивых ноче́й
Прозра́чный су́мрак, блеск безлу́нный,
50 Когда́ я в ко́мнате мое́й
Пишу́, чита́ю без лампа́ды,
И я́сны спя́щие грома́ды
Пусты́нных у́лиц, и светла́
Адмиралте́йская игла́,
И не пуска́я тьму́ ночну́ю
На золоты́е небеса́,
Одна́ заря́ смени́ть другу́ю
Спеши́т, дав но́чи полчаса́.[2]
Люблю́ зимы́ твое́й жесто́кой
60 Недви́жный во́здух и моро́з,
Бег са́нок вдоль Невы́ широ́кой,
Деви́чьи ли́ца я́рче роз,
И блеск и шум и го́вор ба́лов,
А в час пиру́шки холосто́й
Шипе́нье пе́нистых бока́лов
И пу́нша пла́мень голубо́й.
Люблю́ вои́нственную жи́вость
Поте́шных Ма́рсовых поле́й,
Пехо́тных ра́тей и коне́й
70 Однообра́зную краси́вость,
В их стро́йно зы́блемом строю́
Лоску́тья сих знамён побе́дных,
Сия́нье ша́пок э́тих ме́дных,
Наскво́зь простре́ленных в бою́.
Люблю́, вое́нная столи́ца,

4

Твоей твердыни дым и гром,
Когда полнощная царица
Дарует сына в царский дом,
Или победу над врагом
80 Россия снова торжествует,
Или, взломав свой синий лёд,
Нева к морям его несёт,
И чуя вешни дни, ликует.

Красуйся, град Петров, и стой
Неколебимо как Россия.
Да умирится же с тобой
И побеждённая стихия;
Вражду и плен старинный свой
Пусть волны финские забудут
90 И тщетной злобою не будут
Тревожить вечный сон Петра!

Была ужасная пора,
Об ней свежо воспоминанье...
Об ней, друзья мои, для вас
Начну своё повествованье.
Печален будет мой рассказ.

ЧАСТЬ ПЕРВАЯ

Над омрачённым Петроградом
Дышал ноябрь осенним хладом.
Плеская шумною волной
100 В края своей ограды стройной,
Нева металась, как больной
В своей постеле беспокойной.
Уж было поздно и темно;
Сердито бился дождь в окно,
И ветер дул, печально воя.
В то время из гостей домой
Пришёл Евгений молодой...
Мы будем нашего героя
Звать этим именем. Оно

110 Звучи́т прия́тно; с ним давно́
Моё перо́ к тому́ же дру́жно.
Прозва́нья нам его́ не ну́жно,
Хотя́ в мину́вши времена́
Оно́, быть мо́жет, и блиста́ло
И под перо́м Карамзина́
В родны́х преда́ньях прозвуча́ло;
Но ны́не све́том и молво́й
Оно́ забы́то. Наш геро́й
Живёт в Коло́мне; где́-то слу́жит,
120 Дичи́тся зна́тных и не ту́жит
Ни о почи́ющей родне́,
Ни о забы́той старине́.

      Ита́к, домо́й прише́д, Евге́ний
Стряхну́л шине́ль, разде́лся, лёг.
Но до́лго он засну́ть не мог
В волне́ньи ра́зных размышле́ний.
О чём же ду́мал он? о том,
Что был он бе́ден, что трудо́м
Он до́лжен был себе́ доста́вить
130 И незави́симость и честь;
Что мог бы Бог ему́ приба́вить
Ума́ и де́нег. Что ведь есть
Таки́е пра́здные счастли́вцы,
Ума́ неда́льнего лени́вцы,
Кото́рым жизнь куда́ легка́!
Что слу́жит он всего́ два го́да;
Он та́кже ду́мал, что пого́да
Не унима́лась; что река́
Всё прибыва́ла; что едва́ ли
140 С Невы́ мосто́в уже́ не сня́ли
И что с Пара́шей бу́дет он
Дни на́ два, на́ три разлучён.
Евге́ний тут вздохну́л серде́чно
И размечта́лся как поэ́т:

      Жени́ться? Ну...заче́м же нет?
Оно́ и тяжело́ коне́чно,
Но что ж, он мо́лод и здоро́в,
Труди́ться день и ночь гото́в;
Он ко́е-как себе́ устро́ит

150 Приют смире́нный и просто́й
И в нём Пара́шу успоко́ит.
«Пройдёт, быть мо́жет, год друго́й –
Месте́чко получу́ – Пара́ше
Препоручу́ хозя́йство на́ше
И воспипта́ние ребя́т...
И ста́нем жить – и так до гро́ба
Рука́ с руко́й дойдём мы о́ба
И вну́ки нас похороня́т...»

Так он мечта́л. И гру́стно бы́ло
160 Ему́ в ту ночь, и он жела́л,
Чтоб ве́тер дул не так уны́ло
И чтобы дождь в окно́ стуча́л
Не так серди́то...
          Со́нны о́чи
Он наконе́ц закры́л. И вот
Реде́ет мгла нена́стной но́чи
И бле́дный день уж настаёт...[3]
Ужа́сный день!
          Нева́ всю ночь
Рвала́ся к мо́рю про́тив бу́ри,
Не одоле́в их бу́йной ду́ри...
170 И спо́рить ста́ло ей не в мочь...
Поу́тру над её брега́ми
Тесни́лся ку́чами наро́д,
Любу́ясь бры́згами, гора́ми
И пе́ной разъярённых вод.
Но си́лой ве́тров от зали́ва
Перегражденная Нева́
Обра́тно шла, гневна́, бурли́ва,
И затопля́ла острова́...
Пого́да пу́ще свирепе́ла,
180 Нева́ вздува́лась и реве́ла,
Котло́м клоко́ча и клубя́сь,
И вдруг, как зверь остервеня́сь,
На го́род ки́нулась. Пред не́ю
Всё побежа́ло, всё вокру́г
Вдруг опусте́ло – во́ды вдруг
Втекли́ в подзе́мные подва́лы,
К решёткам хлы́нули кана́лы,
И всплыл Петро́поль как Трито́н,
По по́яс в во́ду погружён.

Оса́да! при́ступ! злы́е во́лны,
Как во́ры, ле́зут в о́кна. Чёлны
С разбе́га стёкла бьют кормо́й.
Лотки́ под мо́крой пеленой,
Обло́мки хи́жин, брёвны, кро́вли,
Това́р запа́сливой торго́вли,
Пожи́тки бле́дной нищеты́,
Грозо́й снесённые мосты́,
Гроба́ с размы́того кладби́ща
Плыву́т по у́лицам!

Наро́д

Зрит Бо́жий гнев и ка́зни ждёт.
Увы́! всё ги́бнет: кров и пи́ща!
Где бу́дет взять?

В тот гро́зный год
Поко́йный царь ещё Росси́ей
Со сла́вой пра́вил. На балко́н,
Печа́лен, сму́тен, вы́шел он
И мо́лвил: «С Бо́жией стихи́ей
Царя́м не совладе́ть». Он сел
И в ду́ме ско́рбными оча́ми
На зло́е бе́дствие гляде́л.

Стоя́ли сто́гны озера́ми
И в них широ́кими река́ми
Влива́лись у́лицы. Дворе́ц
Каза́лся о́стровом печа́льным.
Царь мо́лвил – из конца́ в коне́ц
По бли́жним у́лицам и да́льным
В опа́сный путь средь бу́рных вод
Его́ пусти́лись генера́лы[4]
Спаса́ть и стра́хом обуя́лый
И до́ма то́нущий наро́д.

Тогда́, на пло́щади Петро́вой,
Где дом в углу́ вознёсся но́вый,
Где над возвы́шенным крыльцо́м
С подъя́той ла́пой, как живы́е,
Стоя́т два льва сторожевы́е,
На зве́ре мра́морном верхо́м,
Без шля́пы, ру́ки сжав кресто́м,
Сиде́л недви́жный, стра́шно бле́дный
Евге́ний. Он страши́лся, бе́дный,
Не за себя́. Он не слыха́л

Как подымался жадный вал,
Ему подошвы подмывая,
Как дождь ему в лицо хлестал,
Как ветер, буйно завывая,
С него и шляпу вдруг сорвал.
Его отчаянные взоры
На край один наведены
Недвижно были. Словно горы,
Из возмущённой глубины
Вставали волны там и злились,
240 Там буря выла, там носились
Обломки...Боже, Боже! там –
Увы! близёхонько к волнам,
Почти у самого залива –
Забор некрашенный, да ива
И ветхий домик: там оне,
Вдова и дочь, его Параша,
Его мечта... Или во сне
Он это видит? иль вся наша
И жизнь ничто, как сон пустой,
250 Насмешка неба над землёй?

И он, как будто околдован,
Как будто к мрамору прикован,
Сойти не может! Вкруг него
Вода и больше ничего!
И обращён к нему спиною
В неколебимой вышине,
Над возмущённою Невою
Стоит с простёртою рукою
Кумир на бронзовом коне.

ЧАСТЬ ВТОРАЯ

260 Но вот, насытясь разрушеньем
И наглым буйством утомясь,
Нева обратно повлеклась,
Своим любуясь возмущеньем
И покидая с небреженьем
Свою добычу. Так злодей,

9

С свире́пой ша́йкою свое́й
В село́ ворва́вшись, ло́мит, ре́жет,
Круши́т и гра́бит; во́пли, скре́жет,
Наси́лье, брань, трево́га, вой!...
270 И грабежо́м отягощённы,
Боя́сь пого́ни, утомлённы,
Спеша́т разбо́йники домо́й,
Добы́чу на пути́ роня́я.

Вода́ сбыла́, и мостова́я
Откры́лась, и Евге́ний мой
Спеши́т, душо́ю замира́я,
В наде́жде, стра́хе и тоске́
К едва́ смири́вшейся реке́.
Но торжество́м побе́ды по́лны,
280 Ещё кипе́ли зло́бно во́лны,
Как бы под ни́ми тлел ого́нь,
Ещё их пе́на покрыва́ла,
И тяжело́ Нева́ дыша́ла,
Как с би́твы прибежа́вший конь.
Евге́ний смо́трит: ви́дит ло́дку;
Он к ней бежи́т как на нахо́дку,
Он перево́зчика зовёт –
И перево́зчик беззабо́тный
Его́ за гри́венник охо́тно
290 Чрез во́лны стра́шные везёт.

И до́лго с бу́рными волна́ми
Боро́лся о́пытный гребе́ц,
И скры́ться вглубь меж их ряда́ми
Всеча́сно с де́рзкими пловца́ми
Гото́в был чёлн – и наконе́ц
Дости́г он бе́рега.
                    Несча́стный
Знако́мой у́лицей бежи́т
В места́ знако́мые. Гляди́т,
Узна́ть не мо́жет. Вид ужа́сный!
300 Всё перед ним завалено́;
Что сбро́шено, что снесено́;
Скриви́лись до́мики, други́е
Совсем обру́шились, ины́е
Волна́ми сдви́нуты; круго́м,

Как бу́дто в по́ле боево́м,
Тела́ валя́ются. Евге́ний
Стремгла́в, не по́мня ничего́,
Изнемога́я от муче́ний,
Бежи́т туда́, где ждёт его́
310 Судьба́ с неве́домым изве́стьем,
Как с запеча́танным письмо́м.
И вот бежи́т уж он предме́стьем,
И вот зали́в, и бли́зок дом...
Что ж э́то?...
Он останови́лся.
Пошёл наза́д и вороти́лся.
Гляди́т...идёт...ещё гляди́т.
Вот ме́сто, где их дом стои́т,
Вот и́ва. Бы́ли здесь воро́ты,
Снесло́ их, ви́дно. Где же дом?
320 И по́лон су́мрачной забо́ты,
Всё хо́дит, хо́дит он круго́м,
Толку́ет гро́мко сам с собо́ю –
И вдруг, уда́ря в лоб руко́ю,
Захохота́л.

Ночна́я мгла́
На го́род тре́петный сошла́;
Но до́лго жи́тели не спа́ли
И меж собо́ю толкова́ли
О дне мину́вшем.
У́тра луч
Из-за уста́лых, бле́дных туч
330 Блесну́л над ти́хою столи́цей,
И не нашёл уже́ следо́в
Беды́ вчера́шней; багряни́цей
Уже́ прикры́то бы́ло зло.
В поря́док пре́жний всё вошло́.
Уже́ по у́лицам свобо́дным
С свои́м бесчу́вствием холо́дным
Ходи́л наро́д. Чино́вный люд,
Поки́нув свой ночно́й прию́т,
На слу́жбу шёл. Торга́ш отва́жный,
340 Не уныва́я, открыва́л
Нево́й огра́бленный подва́л,
Сбира́ясь свой убы́ток ва́жный

11

На бли́жнем вы́местить. С дворо́в
Свози́ли ло́дки.

        Граф Хвосто́в,
Поэ́т, люби́мый небеса́ми,
Уж пел бессме́ртными стиха́ми
Несча́стье Не́вских берего́в.

        Но бе́дный, бе́дный мой Евге́ний...
Увы́! Его́ смяте́нный ум
350 Про́тив ужа́сных потрясе́ний
Не устоя́л. Мяте́жный шум
Невы́ и ве́тров раздава́лся
В его́ уша́х. Ужа́сных дум
Безмо́лвно по́лон, он скита́лся.
Его́ терза́л како́й-то сон.
Прошла́ неде́ля, ме́сяц — он
К себе́ домо́й не возвраща́лся.
Его́ пусты́нный уголо́к
Отда́л в наймы́, как вы́шел срок,
360 Хозя́ин бе́дному поэ́ту.
Евге́ний за свои́м добро́м
Не приходи́л. Он ско́ро све́ту
Стал чужд. Весь день броди́л пешко́м,
А спал на при́стани; пита́лся
В око́шко по́данным куско́м.
Оде́жда ве́тхая на нём
Рвала́сь и тле́ла. Злы́е де́ти
Броса́ли ка́мни вслед ему́.
Неред́ко кучерски́е пле́ти
370 Его́ стега́ли, потому́
Что он не разбира́л доро́ги
Уж никогда́; каза́лось — он
Не примеча́л. Он оглушён
Был шу́мом вну́тренней трево́ги.
И так он свой несча́стный век
Влачи́л, ни зверь ни челове́к,
Ни то ни сё, ни жи́тель све́та,
Ни при́зрак мёртвый...

             Раз он спал
У Не́вской при́стани. Дни ле́та
380 Клони́лись к о́сени. Дыша́л
Нена́стный ве́тер. Мра́чный вал

Плескал на пристань, ропща пени
И бьясь об гладкие ступени,
Как челобитчик у дверей
Ему не внемлющих судей.
Бедняк проснулся. Мрачно было:
Дождь капал, ветер выл уныло,
И с ним вдали во тьме ночной
Перекликался часовой...
390 Вскочил Евгений; вспомнил живо
Он прошлый ужас; торопливо
Он встал; пошёл бродить и вдруг
Остановился, и вокруг
Тихонько стал водить очами
С боязнью дикой на лице.
Он очутился под столбами
Большого дома. На крыльце
С подъятой лапой, как живые,
Стояли львы сторожевые,
400 И прямо в тёмной вышине
Над ограждённою скалою
Кумир с простёртою рукою
Сидел на бронзовом коне.

    Евгений вздрогнул. Прояснились
В нём страшно мысли. Он узнал
И место, где потоп играл,
Где волны хищные толпились,
Бунтуя злобно вкруг него,
И львов, и площадь, и Того,
410 Кто неподвижно возвышался
Во мраке медною главой,
Того, чьей волей роковой
Под морем город основался...
Ужасен он в окрестной мгле!
Какая дума на челе!
Какая сила в нём сокрыта!
А в сем коне какой огонь!
Куда ты скачешь, гордый конь,
И где опустишь ты копыта?
420 О мощный властелин судьбы!
Не так ли ты над самой бездной,
На высоте, уздой железной
Россию поднял на дыбы?[5]

Кругóм поднóжия куми́ра
Безýмец бéдный обошёл
И взóры ди́кие навёл
На лик держáвца полуми́ра.
Стесни́лась грудь егó. Челó
К решётке хлáдной прилеглó,
430 Глазá подёрнулись тумáном,
По сéрдцу плáмень пробежáл,
Вскипéла кровь. Он мрáчен стал
Пред горделúвым истукáном
И, зýбы сти́снув, пáльцы сжав,
Как обуя́нный си́лой чёрной,
«Добрó, строи́тель чудотвóрный! –
Шепнýл он, злóбно задрожáв, –
Ужó тебé!...» И вдруг стремглáв
Бежáть пусти́лся. Показáлось
440 Емý, что грóзного царя́,
Мгновéнно гнéвом возгоря́,
Лицó тихóнько обращáлось...
И он по плóщади пустóй
Бежи́т и слы́шит за собóй –
Как бýдто грóма грохотáнье –
Тяжело-звóнкое скакáнье
По потрясённой мостовóй.
И озарён лунóю блéдной,
Простёрши рýку в вышинé,
450 За ним несётся Всáдник Мéдный
На звóнко скáчущем конé;
И во всю ночь, безýмец бéдный
Кудá стопы́ ни обращáл,
За ним повсю́ду Всáдник Мéдный
С тяжёлым тóпотом скакáл.

И с той поры́, когдá случáлось
Идти́ той плóщадью емý,
В егó лицé изображáлось
Смятéнье. К сéрдцу своемý
460 Он прижимáл поспéшно рýку,
Как бы егó смиря́я мýку,
Картýз изнóшенный сымáл,
Смущённых глаз не подымáл
И шёл сторóнкой.

Óстров мáлый
На взмóрье вúден. Иногдá
Причáлит с нéводом тудá
Рыбáк на лóвле запоздáлый
И бéдный ýжин свой варúт,
Или чинóвник посетúт,
470 Гуляя в лóдке в воскресéнье,
Пустынный óстров. Не взрослó
Там ни былúнки. Наводнéнье
Тудá, игрáя, знаеслó
Домúшко вéтхий. Над водóю
Остáлся он, как чёрный куст.
Его прошéдшею веснóю
Свезлú на бáрке. Был он пуст
И весь разрýшен. У порóга
Нашлú безýмца моегó,
480 И тут же хлáдный труп его
Похоронúли рáди Бóга.

ПРИМЕЧÁНИЯ А.С. ПУ́ШКИНА

1. Альгарóтти гдé-то сказáл: 'Pétersbourg est la fenêtre par laquelle la Russie regarde en Europe'.

2. Смотрú стихú кн. Вяземского к графúне З***.

3. Мицкéвич прекрáсными стихáми описáл день, предшествовáвший Петербýргскому наводнéнию, в однóм из лýчших своúх стихотворéний Oleszkiewicz. Жаль тóлько, что описáние его не тóчно. Снéгу нé было – Невá не былá покрыта льдом. Нáше описáние вернéе, хотя в нём и нет ярких крáсок пóльского поэ́та.

4. Граф Милорáдович и генерáл-адъютáнт Бенкендóрф.

5. Смотрú описáние пáмятника в Мицкéвиче. Онó займствовано из Рубáна – как замечáет сам Мицкéвич.

TEXTUAL NOTES

References in bold throughout are to line numbers.

Title page (p. 1)

Ме́дный вса́дник: the eminent scholar Roman Jakobson has observed that whereas Pushkin habitually used reference to person(s) or setting for the titles of his major works, *The Bronze Horseman* is one of three late pieces in which the title refers instead to a statue and the material from which it is made. (The other two are *The Stone Guest* [*Ка́менный гость*] and *The Tale of the Golden Cockerel* [*Ска́зка о золото́м петушке́*], from Pushkin's other two 'Boldino autumns' of 1830 and 1834.) The statue is in each case endowed with a 'supernatural, unfathomable power'. It comes to life; and its intervention leads to the death of a leading male character, whose resistance is in vain (Jakobson, pp. 4-7 ff.).[*]

A comparable association by title links *The Bronze Horseman* and *The Stone Guest* with *The Queen of Spades* (*Пи́ковая да́ма*, 1833). All three Russian titles comprise two words: a noun which ordinarily designates a living person, and an accompanying adjective which 'de-animates' that person. The referent is not the less-than-admirable 'hero' but his antagonist, best understood as a composite entity: part human-now-(or soon-to-be)-deceased, part posthumous representation in inert form, part uncanny reanimation (or seeming reanimation), with overtones of a vengeful instrument of fate. The supernatural is most prominent in *The Queen of Spades*, which culminates in madness; and least emphatic in *The Stone Guest*, which ends with death but not madness. *The Bronze Horseman* combines these ingredients.

A number of Soviet and recent Western critics have taken the occurrence of ме́дный instead of бро́нзовый in Pushkin's title to contain an element of demeaning irony: the substitution of hollow, reddish 'copper' for the resonant, noble 'bronze' from which Peter's statue is truly cast. The argument is erroneous. In Russian odes of the 18th and early 19th centuries, ме́дный was habitually used to designate 'bronze', and for

---

[*] It is not a purpose of these Notes to provide detailed scholarly reference to secondary literature. *Direct quotation* of critical sources is, however, generally given precise attribution: by author's name and page number, where the work appears in the Bibliography; or by fuller reference in a few cases where inclusion in the select Bibliography seemed inappropriate.

Pushkin's contemporaries the two words were broadly synonymous. Мéдный, however, was elevated and poetic, брóнзовый was stylistically neutral: technically precise but unpoetic.

Петербу́ргская по́весть: in modern Russian, по́весть denotes a prose narrative longer than a short story (расска́з) but less complex than a novel (рома́н). In Pushkin's time it was used primarily of a romantic verse tale with exotic setting, such as his *Captive of the Caucasus* (*Кавка́зский пле́нник*, 1821). The combination with non-romantic петербу́ргский would have struck an unconventional note, in keeping with the mature Pushkin's conscious orientation away from romantic tradition toward the real, the contemporary and 'prosaic'. In place of the typical romantic hero, noble and exceptional, his innovatory 'Petersburg tale' (after a prelude which draws on the pre-realist, pre-romantic conventions of classicism!) will accordingly depict an unassuming, emphatically ordinary 'hero'.

At the same time, it is possible that Pushkin perceived the term по́весть as a translation of the French *conte* – and was aware of its identity in sound to the word *compte* (account, score). By a bilingual pun typical of Pushkin's later work, his subtitle might thereby carry a secondary meaning of an account rendered, a 'settling of scores' with Petersburg and all it represented.

Foreword (p. 2)

Происше́ствие...*В. Н. Бе́рхом*: the reference is to *A Detailed Historical Account of All the Floods that Have Occurred in Saint Petersburg* (*Подро́бное истори́ческое изве́стие о всех наводне́ниях, бы́вших в Санктпетербу́рге*, published 1826), compiled by the prolific author and naval engineer Vasilii Nikolaevich Berkh. This included a lengthy contribution on the flood of 1824, in the form of an eyewitness account by Pushkin's enemy, the writer and police informant Faddei Bulgarin. Pushkin took a copy of Berkh's pamphlet with him to Boldino in 1833, and drew extensively on the article by Bulgarin (whom he avoids naming) at several points in his poem.

Pushkin's Foreword reinforces the spirit of his subtitle, Петербу́ргская по́весть, in its insistence on authentic realism. It is also polemically barbed. The work of Berkh-Bulgarin was propagandistic as well as documentary, designed to stem criticism of the city's location (and hence of Imperial lack of judgement), and allay contemporary fears of worse calamities to come. It played down the exceptional nature of the 1824 disaster (comparable disasters occurred in other countries); and strongly emphasised the 'rapid and effective measures' of present tsar and government in 'averting the potentially devastating consequences of inundation: poverty and disease'. In the 'unofficial' tale of Evgenii's fate, Pushkin's 'truth' (и́стина) is somewhat grimmer.

By stressing his reliance on contemporary journals, Pushkin would also have been mindful of his own relation to Imperial authority. One unspoken implication was that his account was above reproach, for it was based on loyalist material already approved by the censor. A contrary implication was that he was unable to draw on first-hand experience of the flood, because in November 1824 he had been in exile at Mikhailovskoe, confined to his father's estate by decree of Alexander I.

8 убо́гого чухо́нца: чухо́нец was a predominantly local, Petersburgian term for the indigenous Karelian Finns settled around the Gulf of Finland. Pushkin's disparaging reference to the 'benighted Finn' conforms with the impressions recorded in 1769 by the English traveller, William Richardson:

> The Finns are neither so tall, nor so handsome as the Russians...
> The poorness of their diet, and the inclement weather to which
> they are so much exposed, give them...a miserable appearance.
> Their language is totally different from that of the Russians;
> ...they are also of a different religion; and though all the
> subjects of the empire may be considered on an equal footing in
> regard to freedom, yet having been conquered by the Russians,
> they are considered as their inferiors. They are accordingly
> treated with the utmost insult and abuse.

An element of Great Russian chauvinism likewise colours the polemic with the Polish poet Adam Mickiewicz which Pushkin conducts through much of *The Bronze Horseman*.

11 (1-11) Стоя́л...гляде́л...ду́мал...: the un-named Peter is introduced by three simple, unprefixed, imperfective verbs. Each is emphasised through a combination of either enjambement or mid-line break with mild syntactic inversion, between verb and pronoun or verb and adverb. A hypermetric stress (see Introduction) on the capitalised Он of l. 2 lends additional weight to the poem's first combination of verb and subject. Each verb, moreover, is carefully interwoven into the sound-texture of the surrounding lines (thus *-oln*, *-ial On*, *-oln*; *dum*, *dal'*, *-iadel*; *u* and *m* each five times, *d* three times in ll. 11-12, etc.). This sonorous 'imperfective' opening powerfully conveys the gravity and deliberacy of Peter's majestic actions, endowing them with a durative, timeless-epic grandeur.

14 (1-14) На берегу́...сосе́ду: A.D.P. Briggs has pointed out that in formal terms the opening ten lines consist of two identical five-line units, rhyming aaBaB. This pattern is most unusual in Pushkin's narrative verse. It is especially striking at the beginning of the poem, where it holds out an unsustained promise of regular stanzaic organisation. In Briggs's view, its introduction and discontinuation create the effect of an 'alien and mystifying' form which is entirely appropriate to the remote natural scene presented in the opening lines. Change ensues from l. 11. As Peter 'begins to think clearly, lay his plans for the future', and 'assume control of the wasteland' before him, so, too, 'the opening "stanza" effect disappears and Pushkin imposes his own familiar order on [the] alien-seeming rhyme-scheme'. Briggs further contends that this formal procedure is tinged with significant irony:

> The exactitude of that opening pattern aaBaB, so carefully chopped off at line five for emphasis, so meticulously repeated up to line ten, suggests an underlying sense of meaningful order which belongs to the natural world as described therein. Peter cannot see it. He must change it, imposing his own rhythms and constructions upon the apparent chaos before him. How wrong he was, both in failing to comprehend the self-enclosed logic of that natural scene and in attempting to destroy it – this is the burden of the whole subsequent story, or a large part of it.
>
> (Briggs, 1991, pp. 128-9)

18-19 по нóвым им волнáм...в гóсти бýдут: им is archaic; для них would be required in modern Russian. In addition to its standard meaning of 'guests', гóсти perhaps retains here its Old Russian meaning of rich (often foreign) merchants. By the seventeenth century, however, the word had evolved to designate specifically the tiny elite of chief merchants who dealt in foreign trade. Peter's reforms brought about their effective ruination; and thus нóвый, too, may be a loaded term, indicating not just Peter's opening-up of the new but also his usurpation of the narrow restrictions of old.

Andrew Kahn points out that бýдут should be understood in the obsolete colloquial sense of 'to frequent, to arrive' (Kahn, p. 44). But this is, in addition, the third occurrence of быть in eight lines (бýдем, бýдет, бýдут). Following the imperfectives of the first paragraph the repetition lends emphatic certainty to Peter's vision, and arguably reinforces the solemn parallel between Peter and the Biblical Creator in the first chapter of Genesis ('And God said, "Let there be light"', etc.).

21 Прошлó сто лет: if the statement is taken literally, the passage of one hundred years from the foundation of St Petersburg would move events on to 1803. Some commentators (perhaps recalling that the statue of the Bronze Horseman was unveiled on the centenary of Peter's ascension to the throne) have preferred to reckon the time-lapse from the year of his death in 1725: a hundred years 'after Peter' would point to the historically fateful year of 1825. More to the point may be the very emphasis on historical reckoning as a part of Peter's legacy (see Introduction p. xx). Symbolically, Peter had even reformed the Russian calendar in December 1699 (or 7208), to follow the lead of 'many European Christian nations' in recording the years from the birth of Christ. Russia had hitherto used the

Byzantine system of reckoning from the supposed creation of the world in 5509 BC.

39-42 И перед мла́дшею...Порфироно́сная вдова́: Nicholas I took exception to these lines in his capacity as Pushkin's personal censor: not least, presumably – though Alexander I's widow had barely survived her husband, and there was no living dowager empress – because of the perceived impropriety of Pushkin's direct reference to the imperial family in formulating a political point. As Nicholas was well aware, the relative merits of Petersburg and Moscow were a common topic of debate in the early 1830s. Moreover, many preferred the cosier, patriarchal informality of 'bright Moscow' (as its advocates often termed it: Pushkin provocatively inverts the accepted formula) to the supposedly cold, bureaucratic atmosphere of his official imperial capital. A secondary issue in this connection was Petersburg's peripheral geographical location and hence, implicitly, the questionable judgement of Nicholas's predecessor in his choice of site.

More broadly, the contrast between 'old' Moscow and 'younger' St Petersburg – roughly speaking, between introverted, mediaeval Muscovy and western-looking, 'modern' Russia – encapsulated the very essence of Peter's reforming endeavours. In consequence, images of 'old' and 'new' are repeatedly though often unobtrusively reformulated throughout Pushkin's poem, always with some bearing on the evaluation of Peter. Here Pushkin's approbation of Moscow's eclipse seems consistent with his sustained eulogy of 'Peter's creation'; but it may be subtly tempered by his use of the adjective порфироно́сная. The etymology of this solemn term for the 'imperial robe' (from Greek *porphuros* – purple) arguably points to the ancient concept of Moscow as the sole legitimate successor to the (Greek) Orthodox-Christian Empire of Byzantium. After the fall of Byzantium (the 'Second Rome') to the infidel Turks in 1453, this was enshrined in the doctrine of Moscow as the 'Third Rome' – the one unalterable bastion of true Orthodox faith. Apologists of Peter the Great and his city, however, made elaborate claims that St Petersburg, too, (re-)constituted Rome – albeit with greater emphasis on the secular, military heritage of the First Rome (consistent with Peter's adoption of the Latinate titles of Imperator, Pater Patriae, etc. in 1721; cf. also the associations with Roman divinities noted below) than on the religious legacy of the Second. Petersburg implicitly 'outshone' faded Moscow as a new, resplendently youthful embodiment of the 'eternal' City of Peter. But the traditional view held that after the Third Rome of Moscow there would be no Fourth. If Moscow was the true (порфироно́сная?) inheritor (now widow) of the Graeco-Byzantine Imperial mantle, then Petersburg was an illegitimate, even chimerical creation (cf. сон Петра́?): a place of apostasy, doomed to perish as a result of divine retribution.

43 Петра́ творе́нье: in its identification of creator with creation, this is perhaps the most significant of the sometimes elaborate circumlocutions by which Pushkin refers to the city. Like his avoidance of Peter's name (used only *in absentia*, in oblique, genitive form: here and in l. 91), this indirectness tends to create an elevated effect of mythical distance. The standard, prosaic name of (Санкт-)Петербу́рг is excluded from the main text of the poem, and occurs only in the adjectival form of the subtitle.

47 Твои́х огра́д узо́р чугу́нный: a reference to the splendid railing of the Summer Garden along the Neva Embankment, erected in 1771-84, though perhaps also, for instance, to the elegantly monumental railings subsequently constructed outside the Kazan Cathedral (1810-11) and the Mikhailovskii Palace (1820s).

Pushkin's expression of aesthetic delight evidently involved an element of polemical rejoinder to the Polish poet A. Mickiewicz, who in the second poem ('The Suburbs of the Capital' ['Przedmieścia Stolica']) of his cycle *The Digression* (*Ustęp*: for a full if somewhat fanciful rhymed translation, see Lednicki, pp. 109-39) had construed the 'iron railings' encircling the lavish residences of the nobility on the outskirts of St Petersburg as a gloomy symbol of constrictive oppression.

50-1 Когда́...чита́ю без лампа́ды: i.e. during St Petersburg's famous 'white nights'. The city is sufficiently far north (6° south of the Arctic Circle) that for a few weeks around mid-summer the sun scarcely sets, and a 'transparent twilight' prevails in place of darkness.

52-3 грома́ды Пусты́нных у́лиц: the adjective is the same as in l. 1. Thus 'waves' are implicitly aligned with 'streets', one of several verbal echoes through which comparison between previous vacuity and subsequent form is maintained. But the 'slumbering masses of desolate streets' perhaps also carries an undertone of glowering menace (грома́ды), or a foretaste of devastation (пусты́нный) and eventual return to the dominance of primal, 'devastating' nature (the пусты́нные во́лны).

54 Адмиралте́йская игла́: the tall, gilded spire of the Admiralty Building. Russian адмиралте́йство has a broader meaning than English 'Admiralty', comprising a complex of shipyard, storehouses and workshops, as well as administrative buildings (Peter also established 'admiralties' in Kronshtadt and Voronezh). The St Petersburg Admiralty was founded as a shipyard in 1704 and fortified the following year. It urgently became the chief birthplace of Peter's Northern Fleet, vital to his intention of 'establishing a firm footing by the sea' (l. 17), and central to his broader military-expansionist ambition. It thus constituted the symbolic heart of 'Peter's creation'. By 1715 it employed 10,000 men, and by the end of his reign had produced over 100 warships and galleys, and nearly 300 smaller vessels.

Peter's original, hurried, wood-and-daub building had been replaced by a sprawling stone factory in 1732-8, and reconstructed on a grand scale during Pushkin's lifetime by A.D. Zakharov, whose graceful neo-classical design of 1806-23 became, as Batiushkov put it, 'the adornment of the city'.

The needle-like spire (игла́) had been incorporated from the beginning. This was a distinctively Petrine architectural feature: a Westernised innovation, alien to the rounded domes and cupolas of Orthodox tradition, and thus (together with the even taller spire of the St Peter and Paul Cathedral) an implicit symbol of the 'Petersburg-Moscow' opposition which Pushkin makes explicit in the previous paragraph. Its golden colour is probably reflected in l. 56 (золоты́е небеса́), where золото́й may be regarded as a transferred epithet.

59-62 Люблю́ зимы́...я́рче роз: in turning from summer to winter, Pushkin again takes issue with Mickiewicz, whose presence one recent Russian scholar claims to detect behind no less than 41 lines of the Introduction (Shvartsband, p. 69). In 'Petersburg', the third poem of *The Digression*, Mickiewicz dwells upon his recurrent theme of winter frost as a hateful symbol of Russia's frozen, lifeless, autocratic oppression; and his satirical invective against things Russian extends to the typical lady of the capital, made unattractive by the cold:

> Her face crab-red and snowy white of hue.

Pushkin, in pointed contrast, asserts his 'love' for the frost, revels in a sense of lively movement and expanse (but note the recurrent juxtaposition of immobility and motion, in ll. 60-1), and celebrates the fresh complexions of young Russian women. Typically, however, his polemical expression of nationalistic pride is itself tinged with ambiguity: his (Petersburg) winter is literally 'cruel'.

64 в час пиру́шки холосто́й: envisaged here is a gathering of the social elite – eligible bachelors such as the hero of Pushkin's novel *Evgenii Onegin*, who regularly dined out, with abundant champagne and punch (and occasional after-dinner excursions to establishments of low repute), in the capital's limited array of fashionable restaurants. In ll. 63-6 Pushkin is thus expressing fond admiration for a 'glittering' social life from which Evgenii, the 'bachelor' of his *Bronze Horseman*, would certainly have been excluded. The passage is double-edged in another sense, too: for by the mid-1830s Pushkin, married since 1831, had wearied of social (and 'bachelor') life. Alone in Petersburg in 1834 he wrote to his wife Natal'ia:

> I turned up at Dumé's [restaurant], where my appearance provoked general merriment: bachelor, bachelor Pushkin! They started plying me with champagne and punch, and asking whether I would go to Sof'ia Astaf'evna's [a well-known brothel]. All this embarrassed me, so that I don't intend going to Dumé's again, and am dining at home....

He had also conceived a strong aversion to the society balls (cf. l. 63) which Natal'ia attended with great enthusiasm and social success, even – to Pushkin's irritation – in her husband's absence. It therefore seems that the sentiments of the poem's narrator were at this point somewhat at odds with the private feelings of the real author. Meaning, even in this overtly most unambiguous of passages, repeatedly proves less stable than first appears.

68 Потéшных Мáрсовых полéй: the 'Field(s) of Mars' (Мáрсово пóле; pluralised by Pushkin) was the largest square in St Petersburg. In Pushkin's day it was completely open, and used, as its name implies (Mars was the Roman god of war), for military drill and parades. It had earlier been a park, bordering on the Summer Gardens, known both as Цари́цын луг ('Tsarina's Meadow', after Peter the Great's wife, Catherine I) and as Потéшное пóле. 'Потéшное' (*obs.*; 'intended for amusement') probably alluded to the fêtes regularly held there. However, these typically included displays of fireworks – enthusiastically adopted and often constructed by Peter himself, and sometimes termed потéшные огни́. Потéшный was also used in the 18th century with reference to mock battles or other military manoeuvres for the 'amusement' of the nobility (after the 'play regiments', потéшные полки́, of Peter's youth). Pushkin, it seems, was indulging here in a piece of tautological ambivalence.

70 (67-70) ...жи́вость...Однообрáзную краси́вость: once again, Pushkin's description involves a polemical response to Mickiewicz's *Digression*. In this case it is a rejoinder to 'The Review of the Army' ('Przegląd wojska'), the longest poem of Mickiewicz's cycle, which is a protracted and harrowing satire on an Imperial military review conducted on the Field of Mars in winter. Several of the participants are left dead on the parade ground. The word однообрáзный alerts to the parallel with Mickiewicz (cf. his: '*Monotonously*, side by side they stand,/Like horses lined up at a trough to eat'); but where the Polish poet found death and grotesque incongruity, Pushkin sees 'liveliness' and 'beauty'.

73-4 Сия́нье шáпок...в бою́: copper helmets were worn by the Life-Guards of the Pavlovsk Regiment; the enemy bullet holes (an oblique hint at the vulnerability of copper/bronze?: other occurrences of мéдный in the poem relate only to Peter's statue) were considered a mark of distinction. The same of course holds for the military standards, tattered in battle.

John Bayley has noted of ll. 68-74 that through traditional phraseology and graceful onomatopoeia, 'Pushkin pulls off the delicate feat of making the martial spectacle seem at once stirring, beautiful, and slightly ridiculous' (Bayley, p. 138).

75-6 Люблю́...дым и гром: the reference is to cannon-fire from the walls of the St Peter and Paul Fortress. Its use to celebrate state occasions had been instituted by decree of Peter.

In one respect, since the Fortress was the point of origin of Peter's 'military capital', this concluding sentence of Pushkin's introductory panegyric relates unobtrusively backwards to the poem's (and city's) beginning, and the present scene confirms the 'triumphant' realisation of Peter's initial strategic vision. Again, however, the very object of Pushkin's admiration renders his praise potentially double-edged. The твердыня (*lit.* firm place: hence looking forward, also, to the theme of 'unshakeability' in the next paragraph) which he extols was not only a fortress, but also a tsarist prison – first used as such by Peter the Great, to incarcerate his own son (contrast l. 78!) and other opponents of his reforms in 1718. More recently, as Pushkin was acutely aware, members of the Decembrist conspiracy whose fate so preoccupied him had been confined and interrogated there by Tsar Nicholas I, before their Siberian exile or execution in 1826. Cannon fire, too, could have negative connotations: shots were fired from the Fortress in warning of disaster as well as celebration – not least, as Berkh-Bulgarin made clear, as the waters rose during the flood of 1824.

For the time being, such undertones of menace remain entirely dormant; but the way is prepared for their activation in the lines that follow.

78 Дарует сына в царский дом: though the image has generalising force, it may include topical reference to the birth of the tsar's third son, Nikolai Nikolaevich, in July 1831. (The tsareviches Aleksandr and Konstantin Nikolaevich had been born in 1818 and 1827; the birth of Nikolai was noted in Pushkin's letters.) The guarantee of dynastic stability within the царский дом of the Romanovs was of pointed significance in the wake of the turbulent events of 1825, when Alexander I had died childless, and Nicholas I, the younger of his two surviving brothers, eventually came to the throne in place of the elder Constantine. The uncertain succession had precipitated a profound crisis: the brief interregnum was the occasion of the Decembrist Revolt.

79-80 Или победу...торжествует: the greatest national victory in living memory was over Napoleon in the 'Patriotic War' of 1812, and it is this which the flags and helmets of the parade in ll. 67-74 most readily evoke. But there may in addition have been a secondary, topical reference to events of summer 1831 – when to Pushkin's approval, and the widespread dismay of the more liberally inclined, Russian armies conclusively crushed revolt in Poland. Pushkin had already drawn parallels between victory over the Poles and the salvation of Russia from Napoleon in his two poems 'To the Slanderers of Russia' ('Клеветникам России') and 'Anniversary of Borodino' ('Бородинская годовщина'; both 1831). A supplementary allusion here (cf. снова) to this recent, narrowly nationalistic 'victory' within the then bounds of the multi-national Russian Empire may seem distasteful, but would be consistent with the spirit of Pushkin's sustained polemic against Adam Mickiewicz.

81-3 Или взломав...ликует: the last three lines of the paragraph appear to involve an unexpected shift in sense, from triumphs of state to the triumph of nature. This is partially concealed by structural parallelism and stylistic uniformity: state-historical and natural events are each incorporated into temporal constructions which are subordinated to a single main verb (люблю, l. 75); and the solemn stylistic register of preceding lines remains unaltered (hence e.g. вёшни, and the rhyme of ликовáть with торжествовáть in l. 83). The implication is perhaps that nature, too, has been successfully accommodated into Peter's triumphant design. Yet the congruence between history and nature is less (or more illusory) than this formal presentation suggests. Взломáть denotes violent action; and the image of the river breaking its constraints is in notable, perhaps unsettling, contrast to its 'stately flow' within well-defined confines at the start of the paragraph (cf. держáвное течéнье, l. 45: the adjective is strongly associated with the power of state and sovereign; one meaning of держáва is 'orb', one of the insignia of royalty). Discontinuity between linear, historical time (прошлó сто лет) and cyclical, natural time (summer, winter, spring), implicit throughout the preceding passage, also increases in prominence here. Thus Pushkin's eulogy of St Petersburg ends disconcertingly. Its still muted note of disquiet is re-articulated in comparable terms behind the following paragraph, and anticipates the 'plot' to come.

84 Красýйся, град Петрóв, и стой: Петрóв is not genitive plural but possessive adjective: 'Peter's'. The second imperative of course looks back to l. 2 of the poem.

86 Да умирúтся же: да is used with present or future verb to mean 'may' in the expression of high-flown sentiment (cf. да здрáвствует... = long live...); же is a particle used for emphasis. Thus 'may the conquered element be reconciled/at peace...'. Here, according to the eminent linguist V.V. Vinogradov, the formula evokes the lofty flavour of the Old Russian chronicles. At the same time the expression of wish must entail the *possibility* of non-fulfilment, and beneath the solemn rhetoric the undertone of latent disquiet is thereby sustained.

Andrew Kahn suggests that this entire paragraph:

> is tantamount to a prayer, almost pagan in its direct supplication of nature and use of the subjunctive: it may be construed as the ritual expression of humility and recognition that, though a semi-deity to his citizens, even Peter the Great and his legacy rely on the benevolence of fate. (Kahn, p. 51)

87 побеждённая стихúя: as well as in its general meaning of 'element(s)', стихúя was used in Pushkin's time as a poeticism for 'sea'. Intriguingly, the stone on which the statue of the Bronze Horseman stands is frequently likened to a wave of the sea: potentially, then, an eloquent representation of 'conquered element', of elemental water transformed into Petrine stone. A more particular secondary connotation of стихúя in the present context may be the spontaneous, unstructured, organic-instinctive qualities which can be associated with traditional Muscovite Orthodoxy, in contrast to the conscious and rational principle of Peter's city.

Note that the vocabulary of victory and enmity, here explicitly applied to natural forces, is that also used in the militaristic contexts of the previous paragraph. Imperial Russia must withstand assault of both kinds.

92 пора: this may refer solely to the time of flood, or more broadly, as Kahn speculates, to the period of 'the Decembrist rebellion and the end of Alexander I's reign' (Kahn, p. 52). Пора rhymes across the paragraph divide with вечный сон Петра, perhaps thereby subtly imparting an unconcluded provisionality to the preceding rhetorical exhortation. The rhyme might also be taken both to underscore a contrast to Peter's grand temporal perspective, yet to imply a linkage between Peter and the story that ensues.

93 Об ней: an obsolete form; о ней in modern Russian.

94 друзья мои: preliminary invocation of the poet's friends was a familiar literary convention, particularly widespread in the romantic narrative poem, and 'friends' is in one respect merely a synonym for 'readers'. But there is also a sense in which *The Bronze Horseman* was indeed addressed to an intimate circle of close friends – alert, for instance, to the complex, private implications of the author's Foreword and Notes. Pushkin may also have had in mind the dedicational poem to Mickiewicz's *Digression*, entitled 'To My Russian [or Muscovite] Friends' ('Do Przyjaciół Moskali'). This included a scathing attack on Pushkin (author of the anti-Polish poems of 1831, here 'Someone, perhaps, seduced by gifts of state...'; 'Perchance with venal tongue he lauds the tyrant...'), to which *The Bronze Horseman* is arguably an elaborate rejoinder. It seems clearer from Pushkin's drafts that the Russian 'friends' alluded to in Mickiewicz's work were now being urged to judge between Mickiewicz and Pushkin – and, of course, to accept the greater accuracy and moral rectitude of the latter.

96 (92-6) Была...рассказ: the Soviet Pushkin scholar S.M. Bondi discovered exact correspondences between the drafts of this paragraph and the dedication to Pushkin's romantic narrative poem of a decade earlier, *The Fountain of Bakhchisarai* (*Бахчисарайский фонтан*, 1823). The details are less pertinent than the attendant indication of an abrupt shift of mode – apparently from odic to romantic – at the point of transition from Introduction to story proper. Such a shift would seem consistent with the romantic appeal to the poet's 'friends', and is ostensibly reinforced both by the adjective ужасный, which might be taken to anticipate a romantic tale of gothic horrors (ужасов: contrast the preceding Люблю...), and by the line Печален будет мой рассказ, which, as the poet Anna Akhmatova realised, echoes the introduction to Byron's poem, *The Giaour*: 'Yet this will be a mournful tale...'. But Pushkin often arouses conventional expectation in order to emphasise his divergence from it. Unlike *The Fountain of Bakhchisarai* or *The Giaour*, the ensuing tale deals, as we have noted, not with distant times and exotic places but with immediate, local events, 'fresh' in the memory. Similarly, Pushkin's hero does not exhibit the passionate, Byronic spiritual grandeur with which romantically-inclined 'reader-friends' might have willingly identified. Tale – and hero – will prove as resolute a departure from high romanticism as from the panegyric of the Introduction.

97-8 Над омрачённым...хлáдом: the tale begins in autumn, with the completion of the natural (a- or anti-historical?) cycle of summer, winter, spring, begun in the Introduction. The high-poetic style (inversion, participle, personification, slavonicism) seems to promise a continuation in the romantic vein introduced in the preceding lines; but a transition to prosaic reality and a direct colloquial register rapidly ensues (e.g. ll. 103-4, 106). The emphasis on autumnal gloom and 'sadness' nevertheless remains.

It is characteristic of the many-sidedness of Pushkin's work – and perhaps a sign of the distance between author and 'non-poet' Evgenii – that in Boldino in 1833 he also wrote the poem 'Autumn' ('Óсень'). There, by contrast, he famously described late autumn as his favourite time of year, invigorating and inspirational.

99 Плескáя: obsolete; плéща (from плескáть: плещý, плéщешь, -ут) would be correct in modern Russian.

102 В...постéле: obsolete; в постéли in modern Russian. This concrete, prosaic simile is in sharp contrast to the apparently aesthetic emphasis of l. 100 (стрóйный), which is still potentially consistent with the terms of the preceding hymn to Peter's achievement (from 'стрóгий, стрóйный вид' to 'Красýйся, град Петрóв', etc.).

107-11 Пришёл Евгéний...давнó...дрýжно: the long familiarity most obviously stems from the novel *Evgenii Onegin*, on which Pushkin had worked from 1823-30, and which was first published in book-form in 1833. He had also used Evgenii as the given name of Ezerskii, hero of the unfinished narrative poem by that title which constituted an important experimental transition between *Onegin* and *The Bronze Horseman*.

As Pushkin was well aware, the name Evgenii which he again chose to adopt derived from the Greek adjective for 'noble'. In 18th-century Russian satire it had become particularly associated with the stock negative figure of the young nobleman who enjoyed all the privileges of his ancestors, but possessed none of their personal merits. In *The Bronze Horseman*, however, the deterioration seems more material than moral.

It may be pertinent, too, that outside the sphere of literary convention, Evgenii had formerly been regarded primarily as a monastic name: appropriate, perhaps, to someone devout in the Orthodox faith, remote, or estranged, from the secular world of the Petrine city.

115 под перóм Карамзинá: Nikolai Mikhailovich Karamzin (1766-1826), one of Pushkin's most important literary predecessors, and author of the multi-volumed *History of the Russian State* (*Истóрия госудáрства Россúйского*, 1818-24, with later supplements). This monumental work ended with the foundation of the Romanov dynasty in 1613. The implication, only slightly attenuated by Pushkin's 'perhaps' (l. 114), is that Evgenii's illustrious family name was firmly rooted in old, Muscovite

Russia, and long antedated the Petrine reforms which had hastened, if not initiated, its eclipse.

118-19 Наш герóй/Живёт в Колóмне: Kolomna was a sprawling and distinctly unfashionable residential area, which extended along the Fontanka Canal to the city outskirts on the Gulf of Finland. It was inhabited primarily by civil servants, tradesman and artisans, increasingly less affluent the further they lived from the centre. A memorably vivid description of the district, 'neither the capital nor the provinces', 'all silence and retirement', was provided soon afterwards by Nikolai Gogol' in his Petersburg story *The Portrait* (*Портрéт*, 1835; revised 1842).

Kolomna had been the setting of Pushkin's previous complete narrative poem, the comic *Little House in Kolomna* (*Дóмик в Колóмне*, 1830). Symptomatically, it was home there to a poor widow and her daughter, probably eking out their living on the meagre pension of a lowly civil servant. Its recurrence in *The Bronze Horseman* should be taken as an indication of Evgenii's equally humble means and social status. For Pushkin's readers, this would not inconceivably have seemed tinged with an element of condescending humour (compare the connotations of any number of unglamorous British place names today). Typically, however, there may also have been an underlying element of pathos – Kolomna was one of the districts worst affected by the flood of 1824 – and even of wry self-projection. Pushkin himself had lived in Kolomna in 1817-20, before the poems he wrote there brought him fame.

122 Ни о забы́той старинé: among the several implications of Evgenii's oblivion, compare and contrast the injunction to the Finnish waves to 'forget' their 'ancient' enmity in ll. 88-9.

123 пришéд: obsolete form of the perfective gerund of прийти́; in modern Russian, compounds of идти́ form their gerund by adding -я to the stem of the future tense (e.g. придя́).

124 Стряхнýл шинéль, раздéлся, лёг: for Pushkin's contemporaries this line, too, would have underscored Evgenii's lowly station: he could afford no servant to take his coat or help him undress.

127 О чём же дýмал он?: a clear echo of 'И дýмал Он' in the opening description of Peter, which invites detailed comparison and contrast between the tsar's велúкие дýмы and Evgenii's more humdrum thoughts. Some notable structural contrasts also underlie the difference in scope of vision: whereas дýмать was forcefully declarative with reference to Peter, here it is interrogative; Peter is introduced by imperfective verbs (and is characterised by them throughout, even in the climactic pursuit scene), Evgenii, in his 'agitation' of mind, is described by a string of perfectives; Peter 'stood', Evgenii 'lay down'; Peter's thoughts are purposefully ordered, Evgenii's 'various' and random; etc.

130 незавúсимость и честь: independence and honour had been fundamental concepts in the system of values which underpinned the 18th-century nobility, but their moral significance has been considerably diluted in Evgenii's consciousness. This doubtless reflects his diminished social status. For Evgenii, in Kahn's view:

'Honour'...means nothing more than the ability to keep his position, and 'independence' is nothing more than sustenance, whereas 'honour' elsewhere in Pushkin can refer to loyalty to a principle, and 'independence' to the historic status of the gentry vis-à-vis the monarch. In this new context, the frankness of an unpoetic word like 'den'gi' is unmistakable.   (Kahn, pp. 55-6)

If this tends to discredit Evgenii, however, it should also be borne in mind that in the summer of 1833 Pushkin himself, from an admittedly less precarious position, had been thinking in similar terms. He had lamented in a letter to the Imperial authorities that he had no permanent source of income apart from his salary as a court official, and that he was consequently obliged to carry out menial duties 'which alone provide me with independence (доставляют мне независимость) and the means to live in Petersburg with my family' (Petersburg was inordinately expensive). He therefore had no time to complete the historical work which he claimed might alleviate his increasing financial need, and secure an untroubled future for himself and his dependants.

Once again, at a point where Pushkin was clearly at pains to distance himself from his character(s), contrary indications of rapprochement also exist.

135 жизнь куда́ легка́: куда́ is here colloquial and ironic, meaning 'so', 'so very'; one of several distinctly unpoetic colloquialisms (cf. e.g. ведь, неда́льнего, едва́ ли...не) which punctuate Evgenii's thoughts in this paragraph.

138-9 река́/Всё прибыва́ла: 'the river was still rising'. Всё + imperfective verb conveys the meaning of persistent duration: i.e. 'to keep on doing something'. Cf. also l. 321.

139-40 едва́ ли/С Невы́ мосто́в уже́ не сня́ли: although by the 1830s there were many stone and wooden bridges across St Petersburg's lesser rivers and canals (cf. l. 36), there was no permanent bridge over the main channel of the Neva (the Больша́я Нева́) until 1850. Instead, two floating bridges of wooden decking were built on pontoons (barges) lying at anchor and secured to the shores. These could be removed in their entirety during the seasonal movement of ice in spring and autumn, or – in theory – whenever the level of the river became dangerously high (an occurrence which Pushkin experienced as he attempted to leave Petersburg for the Urals and subsequently Boldino in August 1833).

The floating bridges were a solution to the problem of traversing a wide and deep river, with powerful currents and heavy flow of ice; but their continuing impermanence perhaps also reflected a resistance to bridge-building inherited from Peter the Great. He had preferred to enforce the proliferation of boats, both large and small; and ferry-craft of various sizes (cf. ll. 285-96) were still much-used even in the early 20th century. By Pushkin's day, the pontoon bridges (sections of which could be removed to allow ships to pass) were nevertheless substantial. Isaakievskii (Isaac's) Bridge, re-designed in 1821, was over twenty metres wide, and boasted twenty or more street-lamps. In 1824, unfortunately, the precautions on which Evgenii speculates were not taken. The bridge was swept away by the flood, and subsequently rebuilt once more.

141 с Парáшей: Парáша is the diminutive form of Прaскóвья. Like Evgenii, it was a name 'familiar to the pen', which Pushkin had used most recently for the resourceful and vivacious heroine of his *Little House in Kolomna*. She too had lived alone with her widowed mother (cf. l. 246), and in relative poverty. But the Parasha of *The Bronze Horseman* lives across the river from Kolomna on Vasil'evskii Island, and unlike in the previous work, her characterisation could scarcely be more meagre. Evgenii's aspirations apart, the sole clues to her being are the dilapidated 'little house' with its unpainted fence (ll. 244-5) and the connotations of her name – inherently Russian, unglamorously un-westernised (cf. Прaскóвья Лáрина, the emphatically Russian-provincial mother of Tat'iana in *Evgenii Onegin*) – perhaps, by the 1830s, already somewhat comically outmoded, most readily associated (especially in the diminutive) with servants (another Parasha is the sprightly maidservant in Pushkin's *Count Nulin* [*Граф Нулин*]) and the hard-pressed under-class of minor officials and tradesmen.

142 Дни нà два, нà три: дни is an obsolete, colloquial genitive singular of день: the correct form in standard modern Russian is дня. The inversion of noun and numeral expresses a somewhat casual approxima-tion: 'for a day or two', lit. 'for two or three days'.

146 Онó: another instance of Evgenii's low-colloquial syntax. In standard Russian the personal pronoun is used relatively only with reference to a preceding noun, with which it must agree in number and gender. Э́то, the neuter form of the demonstrative pronoun э́тот, must be used to refer to a preceding statement or concept (in this case, the notion of marriage).

148 Трудúться день и ночь готóв: it is worth noting that the aspira-tion to self-advancement through hard work was itself a reflection of social class. The more privileged members of society – the ленúвцы of ll. 133-4 – frequently lived in considerable and perpetual debt: such a course was not open to the likes of Evgenii.

153 Местéчко: the diminutive of мéсто, here used solely in the sense of 'job', 'position': the implication is of (relative) security, but the diminutive limits the scope of Evgenii's ambition. A number of English-language commentators are mistaken in taking местéчко to mean 'little place', in the sense of place of residence.

154 Препоручу́ хозя́йство на́ше: the most conspicuous example of a stilted bureaucratic element (cf. also месте́чко and the phrase Прию́т смире́нный и просто́й) which serves, in addition to the colloquialisms already noted, to characterise Evgenii through his language. Although nothing is shown of his work as a government clerk, his relation to that sphere is clearly suggested by his manner of expression.

159-67 И гру́стно бы́ло/Ему́ в ту ночь...Ужа́сный день!: the passage contains a further example of Pushkin's persistent play with literary genre and conventional expectation. The description of Evgenii's nocturnal mood in ll. 159-63 clearly echoes that of John Melmoth's sensations at the end of the second chapter of Charles Maturin's archetypal 'tale of terror', *Melmoth the Wanderer*:

> as the wind sighed round the desolate apartment, and the rain pattered with a mournful sound against the dismantled window, [John] wished – what did he wish for? – he wished the sound of the wind less dismal, and the dash of the rain less monotonous. He may be forgiven, it was past midnight, and there was not a human being awake but himself within ten miles....

But Pushkin's subsequent use of the adjective ужа́сный (which, as we have seen, was strongly associated with the essentially nocturnal genre of gothic-romantic horror) here relates not, as might be anticipated, to night but to 'pale day': the у́жас to which he turns is a concrete matter not of the romantic imagination, but of stark, waking reality.

The conjunction of this 'anti-romantic' twist with Pushkin's third authorial footnote suggests that the particular target of his polemic was less romanticism in general than, once more, Adam Mickiewicz. He refutes Mickiewicz's grand-romantic, prophetic-apocalyptic interpretation of the flood of 1824 as inevitable, justly deserved national catastrophe, and does so, in part, on the level of aesthetic (literary-generic) principles.

171-4 Поу́тру...разъярённых вод: in seeming accord with the concern for accuracy expressed in Pushkin's Foreword and third footnote, the description of the flood in this paragraph and the next relies extensively on contemporary sources. The present sentence is a dazzling poetic trans-formation of the following passage from Berkh:

> around 10 o'clock in the morning, as the water gradually in-creased, crowds of curious onlookers made for the banks of the Neva, which was rising high in foaming waves (высоко́ воздыма́лось пе́нистыми волна́ми) and smashing them with terrible sound and spray (бры́згами) against the granite banks.

175-87 Но си́лой ве́тров...хлы́нули кана́лы: as noted in The Petersburg Background (p. xxxvi) the immediate cause of the flood is that the swollen waters of the Neva are held in check by the contrary flow of the sea, driven inward by the wind and storm. Forced back, the river bursts its banks.

Pushkin continues to exploit details drawn from Berkh:

> [From the shores of the Gulf of Finland] the boundless expanse of the waters seemed a boiling abyss (кипя́щею пучи́ною), across which stretched a fog formed from the spray of the waves (бры́зги волн), driven against the current and broken into roaring vortices (реву́щими ви́хрями). White foam swirled (клуби́лась) over the towering watery masses, which grew incessantly and finally rushed frenziedly (я́ростно) for the shore.

And, from a different vantage point:

> The Neva, encountering an obstacle (препя́тствие) to its flow and being unable to empty itself into the sea, swelled within its banks, filled the canals, and gushed (хлы́нула) through the underground pipes onto the streets in the form of fountains. In a single moment the water poured over the sides of the embankments, from the rivers and all the canals, and flooded the streets...Cellars (погреба́), basements (подва́лы) and all lower stories were immediately filled with water. Everyone saved what they could...Meanwhile, the crowds that had been on the streets rushed for the houses....

The underground pipes referred to were covered by iron grilles (решётки).

181 Котло́м клоко́ча и клубя́сь: the factual (or at any rate, journalistic) basis of Pushkin's description by no means precludes the possibility of symbolic interpretation. The critic B.M. Gasparov, for instance, has recently taken this famously alliterated line to intimate the dark stirrings of hell, possibly as volcanic eruption: the first in a series of metaphors, including malicious attack by wild beast, thieves, military enemy and robber bands, to imply the unleashing of the chaotic or demonic underground forces which lurk behind Peter's cosmic-divine creation (Gasparov, p. 292).

183 Пред не́ю: the first of the poem's three unrhymed lines (see also ll. 331 and 364). The absence of this rhyme has sometimes been explained as an oversight due to the speed with which Pushkin re-worked his final manuscript(s), for the first draft contained a rhyming line subsequently omitted. But the enjambement lends the unrhymed preposition + pronoun unusual emphasis, and the explanation offered in a detailed study of Pushkin's rhyming practice by the American scholar J.T. Shaw might seem more plausible:

If Pushkin had not cancelled the line with the rhymeword to go with пред нéю, the passage would have consisted of a chain of six consecutive couplet rhymes. The nonrhyme is *almost* the exact centre of a sequence of couplets, and disrupts the harmonious structure of the passage (intentionally, one suspects), as a sort of metaphor of the flood disharmoniously 'assaulting' St Petersburg.

(J. Thomas Shaw, *Pushkin's Poetics of the Unexpected*
[Columbus, Ohio: Slavica, 1993], p. 72)

188-9 И всплыл...погружён: Triton is the merman or sea-god of Greek myth, the upper half of his body that of a man, the lower that of a fish or dolphin.

Consistently with the Greek form 'Petropolis' in place of the essentially Christian 'Peter's city' (град Петрóв), we might discern here the continuing 'surfacing' of the created city's pagan substratum, a menacingly chaotic inversion of the world order. Alternatively, the appearance of the Triton in Pushkin's story of devastating flood could suggest a parallel to the Roman poet Ovid's version of the cataclysmic world flood in Book 1 of *Metamorphoses*. In Ovid, Triton is summoned by his master, Neptune (incidentally, like Mars, a deity both favoured by and iconographically associated with Peter the Great). He rises from the deep to signal the seas to return to their shores and the swollen rivers to their allotted channels. His appearance at the high point of the flood thus heralds its eventual end and the gradual restoration of the desolated earth/world.

In the face of such conflicting interpretational possibilities, the observations of A. Ospovat and R. Timenchik may have much to commend them:

> Unified by five stressed o's and [consonantal] repetitions ('pl', 'tr' and others), [the couplet] brings together the opening and closing verbal forms, which signify oppositely directed actions. The endless fluctuation of meaning between the two antonyms at either end of the couplet depicts the play of the Triton in the waves of the Neva. The elegant poetic dialectic of the two-line miniature forces us time and again to retrace the circle from end to beginning.   (Ospovat and Timenchik, p. 244)

It could further be argued that this represents a pivotal encapsulation of the whole, or *mise en abyme*: for a similar pattern might be detected on a larger scale in the interplay between the end and beginning of the entire poem, between chaotic devastation and cosmic construction. But it should be added that the two lines constitute an abrupt switch of tone at the emphatic end of the verse paragraph. Typically, in the insertion of this archaising literary flourish into the dramatic, realistic description, there is perhaps an element of humorous play, liable to undermine any single, serious interpretation.

190-9 Осáда!...Плывýт по ýлицам!: whereas the previous paragraph was dominated by a plethora of verbal forms in past tense narrative, Pushkin now switches to the present, and a list of nouns. Several items of this 'catalogue' (a favourite Pushkinian device) could have been suggested by Berkh; others by S. Aller, whose *Description of the Flood which Took Place in St Petersburg on the Seventh Day of November 1824* (*Описáние наводнéния, бы́вшего в Санктпетербýрге 7 числá ноября́ 1824 г.*; 1826) referred not only to the 'roofs of houses, wood and other rubbish' floating along or blocking the streets, but also to tradesmen's wares, remains of some of the city's wooden bridges and even 'many wooden crosses from graves and so forth', washed from the Smolenskoe Cemetery. The grisly detail of the coffins had already appeared in a poem by Anna Volkova published in the aftermath of the flood (see Kahn, p. 59). It perhaps evokes once more the notion of the flood as apocalyptic upheaval or Last Judgement, which the poem seems persistently to dismiss, yet just as persistently to reintroduce for more or less serious consideration. Gutsche, however, sees the detail an an allusion to Decembrism (Gutsche, p. 28).

199-202 Нарóд...Где бýдет взять?: l. 200 uses elevated linguistic register to convey, once more, a perception of the flood as divine retribution: not, however, as the unique insight of a lone romantic prophet – such as Mickiewicz's mystically and Biblically-inclined Oleszkiewicz (see Pushkin's third footnote) – but as the implicitly more commonplace, even banal reaction of 'the people'. The authority of the reference to divine anger is also potentially (but not absolutely!) compromised in what follows, by juxtaposition to a different viewpoint, expressed through an abrupt stylistic shift to what is presumably an alternative idiom of 'the people': colloquial interjection, emphasised by the hypermetrical (additional) stress on всё; and the still more colloquial, elliptical phrase где бýдет взять? (roughly equivalent to 'where can they be got'; a more standard sentence might be formed by addition of verbal auxiliary and direct object: где мóжно бýдет их взять?). In place of passively fatalistic apprehension of the terrible cataclysm, this question conveys a switch of focus beyond the falsely imagined 'End', and an albeit tentative practical concern with survival and how to cope. A note of despair nevertheless remains (to accept the need for remedy is of course by no means to achieve one); and in this there may be a further, polemical point. The semi-official formula кров и пи́ща possibly echoes Berkh, where it constituted a glib diminution of the scope of the disaster for propagandistic purposes: 'Within the first twenty-four hours there was not a single person in the capital without food and shelter (без пи́щи и крóва)'. Pushkin believed otherwise, and was privately scathing of the government's inability to provide the ordinary people (нарóд) with appropriate relief. (On 4 December 1824, for instance, he wrote to his brother of a recent distribution of cash: 'a million roubles is all very well, but what about salt and bread and oats and wine? in winter it would be no sin to think about that...'.)

Both the contrasting play of active and passive responses and the consideration of the efficacy of (official) relief measures persist through the remainder of the paragraph.

203-4 Покойный царь...Со славой правил: Alexander I, who reigned from 1801-25. The early years of Alexander's reign brought hope of enlightened liberal reform, but after the Napoleonic wars – as Pushkin, who had been exiled by him in 1820, seemed to concur – his rule was increasingly characterised by personal weakness, religious mysticism and obscurantism. Со славой, as the immediate lexical context confirms, is potentially ironic; покойный serves to recall that Alexander had almost exactly one more year to live (the mortality of tsars?), and possibly brings to mind superstitious associations of his fate with the city's floods. In the poem's drafts Pushkin had linked Alexander's birth in 1777 to the great flood of that year, with an implication of further misfortunes to come. Popular (and literary: cf. Mickiewicz) imagination likewise readily interpreted the flood of 1824 as an omen of Alexander's imminent demise.

205 Печален, смутен: in modern Russian, the long form would be required when, as here, an adjective is used in apposition (i.e. separated by commas from a main-clause noun or pronoun – in this instance он – which it qualifies and expands without affecting the grammatical structure of the main sentence).

206 Божией: in modern Russian, Божий belongs to the group of possessive adjectives in -ий with stems in -ь in all forms except the masculine nom./acc. sg.: thus the correct form here would be Божьей. Pushkin's full-vocalic -и increases the line's assonantal richness while lending archaic gravity to the tsar's utterance.

207 (204-7) На балкон...не совладеть: the episode of the tsar's appearance on the balcony of the Winter Palace was probably suggested to Pushkin by a then unpublished eye-witness account by his acquaintance, the author A.S. Griboedov, which he could have read when both were in Petersburg in 1828 (Izmailov, ed., pp. 116-20). Griboedov places the tsar on the balcony at a 'fateful moment' which saw the destruction of the main bridges, the sinking of several ships, and people clinging for their lives onto the trees of main thoroughfares. The words attributed to Alexander may have their source in his reaction to the flood in a letter to N.M. Karamzin of 10 November 1824, which Pushkin could have known of from mutual friends of the recipient: 'My duty is to be here: I would account my absence a fault. ...It is the will of God (воля Божия): we can only bow our heads before it'.

It should be noted that the use of Бóжией aligns the tsar's mystical fatalism with that of the нарóд in l. 200; and that the element(s) are at this point in the poem associated with the divine.

207-9 сел…глядéл: the second verb is of course also used of the poem's other, un-named, 'deceased' tsar, as he looks in thought (дýма/дýмы) across a watery expanse at the start of the poem, in l. 3. (In comparable fashion, the immediately subsequent image of the imperial dwelling-place as 'sad island' in ll. 213-14 will initiate a resonance with the very last lines of the poem.) Irrespective of which posture (if either) is ultimately more justified, it is one of several telling points of contrast that whereas Peter, Pushkin's 'powerful lord of fate' (мóщный властелúн судьбы́; l. 420), was shown 'standing' in unhesitating contemplation of future construction, his heir Alexander, here in apparent impotent subservience to 'fateful' forces, is instead shown 'sitting' in anguished contemplation of present destruction (compare also ll. 6-7 with ll. 211-12).

215 дáльным: an obsolete form. In modern Russian, дáльний (far, distant) is a soft adjective.

220 Тогдá: the implicit temporal connection of Evgenii's predicament with the events of the preceding paragraph continues to reflect satirically on the efforts of the rescuers (the unrescued Evgenii is stranded virtually in sight of the Winter Palace balcony); but a more serious significance perhaps lies in the simultaneity of his reappearance with foregoing thoughts of divine retribution, refocussed in implicit reproach of Peter.

220-1 на плóщади…нóвый: Peter's Square was more generally known as Senate Square (Сенáтская плóщадь), although it had been officially renamed after the unveiling of his statue in 1782; subsequently Decembrist Square (плóщадь Декабрúстов). Site of the Bronze Horseman, and of the Decembrist Revolt. The 'new house' at its corner – now No. 12, Admiralty Prospect – had been built for Prince A.Ia. Lobanov-Rostovskii (1788-1866), to the design of August Montferrand, architect of St Isaac's Cathedral, in 1817-20. An eight-columned portico rises from first-floor level (cf. под столбáми; l. 396); two large marble lions mounted on high plinths flank the stairway from the street to a lofty arcaded porch enclosing the main entrance. Since Pushkin's time, the house has sunk, and the street-level has risen significantly. Evgenii's vantage point was higher than it now appears.

225-7 На звéре…Сидéл: Evgenii's location may have been suggested to Pushkin by a contemporary anecdote concerning one Iakovlev, who had been viewing the rising waters of the Neva and found himself suddenly cut off by the flood. He sought refuge by climbing onto one of the lions at the entrance to the Lobanov mansion, where he was forced to remain until the waters subsided. An echo of the comic aspect of this predicament might be detected in l. 231. Yet Pushkin may also have been grimly aware that a year later the same Lobanov Mansion had also provided Nicholas with a vantage point from which to survey the Decembrists' insubordination, and was the spot from which he gave the order for his troops to fire their cannon at the rebellious forces.

Evgenii's posture, however, may evoke quite different resonances, symbolic once more of the opposition between ancient, Orthodox Muscovy and new, secular (or pagan) Petersburg. Bethea points out that the lion – with a silver cross in its right paw, denotative of an Orthodox mission – was the heraldic emblem of Iurii Dolgorukii, founder of Moscow. Evgenii – the (barely) surviving lone heir of the 'old' nobility (ll. 112-22), now depicted astride the marble lion with raised paw, his arms symbolically 'crossed', arguably linked in time (тогда) with the preceding apprehensions of a divine will – is implicitly elevated to the status of (unwitting) knight-champion of the traditional Muscovite order. But he remains, of course, an incongruous and ignominious 'horseman'(!), and the sorry pathos of his position perhaps suggests that the symbolic religious-historical conflict is so unequal as to have already lost all practical substance. Evgenii – the descendant of ancient noble lineage recast as humble (Petrine) civil servant – is now captive in 'Peter's' space (на площади Петровой), where he is obliged to sit on watch outside the новый дом, rather than the ветхий домик of Parasha and her mother (so 'ancient' it has fallen into disrepair) that he would wish instead to protect. He seems at this point as impotent as he is 'immobile', while the very lions which, as Bethea puts it, 'should be guarding [cf. сторожевы́е] the traditions of "old" Russia' have been similarly 'transplanted to the camp of the enemy' (Bethea, pp. 113-14).

227-8 стра́шно бле́дный...страши́лся: the last two paragraphs of Part 1 are even more than usually replete with all manner of verbal repetition, both lexical, as here (cf. also e.g., подъя́тый/подыма́лся, завыва́я/вы́ла, недви́жный/недви́жно, возмущённой/возмущённою, etc.), and syntactic (где...где..., как...как..., там...там..., etc.). One theory is that such repetitive accumulation reflects the increasing turmoil in Evgenii's mind. At the same time, however, the passage is no less laden with multiple verbal echoes and anticipations which seem to condense and recapitulate much of the remainder of the poem: from the river of l. 4 (cf. носи́лись, l. 240; note also the continuing opposition of стоя́ть–сиде́ть in ll. 258 and 227), through the architectural splendour of the Introduction (cf. the vocabulary of ll. 220-3), the worsening weather as Evgenii returns home (cf. ll. 232 ff.; compare even the missing hat with the earlier discarded coat), the 'evil' waves and flotsam (обло́мки) of the flood itself (239-41), and the mixed register of the people's alternating thoughts of God and practicalities (cf. 241-2); and onward, to anticipate what Evgenii will encounter (or not) across the waters (ll. 243-5), and his final confrontation with the statue (cf. ll. 223-4; 251-9). The list is of course by no means exhaustive. Certain of these repetitions are discussed in detail by Kahn, who notes Pushkin's characteristic fondness for 'redescription and renaming' as a way of creating 'multiple view-points', 'secondary meaning' and 'ominous connotations'.

235-6 взóры/На крáй одúн наведенЫ́: from his elevated vantage point Evgenii would have looked across the emptiness of Peter's Square and the Neva beyond, to the shore of Vasil'evskii Island. (Nowadays the view is obscured by trees.) His 'despair' would have been caused not least by the realisation that Isaac's Bridge, which ran directly from the Square to the Island, had been washed away. Parasha and her mother can be presumed to have lived in the poor wooden housing 'close to the waves, almost on the Gulf itself' (ll. 242-3), on the Island's northern or western extremities. It suffered particularly severe damage from the flood.

245 онé: obsolete feminine plural form of the personal pronoun. Онú in modern Russian.

248-50 иль вся...землёй?: it is perhaps unclear whether this arch-romantic sentiment is that of the narrator (notwithstanding the preceding polemic with the romanticism of Mickiewicz), or belongs solely to Evgenii – who was last seen before this at the moment where he closed his сóнны óчи (though the present lines also invite contrast and comparison with вéчный сон Петрá in l. 91), but whose previous associations with the romantic hero had seemed merely parodic. (Even his depiction alone and motionless against the storm parodies a frequent posture of the Byronic hero, with counterparts in Pushkin's own romantic narrative poems of the early 1820s, *The Captive of the Caucasus* and *Vadim.*) The issue of point of view, which is henceforth persistently, unsettlingly problematic (is кумúр in l. 259, for instance, the perception of Evgenii or narrator?), becomes most acute during the horseman's dramatic pursuit of Evgenii (the objective presentation of a fantastic/supernatural reality, or a madman's delusion?).

255 обращён к немý спинóю: whatever larger significance is read into the image of the statue at this point, much has naturally been made of this pose as a sign of utter indifference to Evgenii and his personal predicament. But even here an alternative reading is not impossible. As Evgenii looks fixedly across the waters, Peter's statue towers imperturbably before him, arm outstretched in resolute confrontation with the elemental flood. From this perspective (though the poet and critic V.F. Khodasevich suggested that the 'terrible' tsar's outstretched arm may have been summoning forth, not calming the demons of the deep), the statue might seem 'unshakeable' precisely in totemic defence of the city and its inhabitants, a (lingering) source of hope and reassurance for the despairing Evgenii, who unconsciously takes what refuge he can behind its protective back. According to this interpretation, at the end of Part 1 Evgenii bears no animosity towards Peter. Only when he learns of Parasha's fate, and so discovers that the 'hope' which he entertains in l. 277 and beyond has been misplaced, is he prompted to the reassessment of attitude which leads to the second, parallel yet altered confrontation with the statue at the poem's culmination. The shift in attitude marks an essential difference between Parts 1 and 2.

259 Кумúр: Pushkin's use of the word for 'idol' (repeated in ll. 402 and 424) evoked the particular displeasure of Nicholas I. Roman Jakobson's observations in connection with the symbolism of the Eastern Church help to elucidate the reason:

> Precisely the Orthodox tradition, which severely condemned the art of sculpture, which did not admit it into churches, and which understood it as a pagan or diabolic device (the two concepts were equivalent for the Church), suggested to Pushkin the close *association of statues with idolatry*, with devilry, with sorcery.
>
> (Jakobson, p. 40)

The latent implication that Peter and his works – and the statue erected to him by Nicholas's grandmother, Catherine – are sacrilegious or demonic is indeed intensified at this point by the suggestion that Evgenii appears bewitched (l. 251). The individual, forgetful of the past and deprived of a future, becomes literally petrified in the province of the pagan idol where, in anticipation of the more protracted intrusion of the supernatural in Part 2, the boundaries between animate and inanimate (lions as well as horses), living and dead, are fluid and interchangeable.

259 (251-9) И он...конé: as the 20th-century poet Georgii Shengeli noted, the first four lines of this paragraph comprise two rhyming couplets, followed by a less regular five-line section (Ospovat and Timenchik, p. 249). The initial pattern leads us to expect an immediate rhyme for спинóю, but Невóю is delayed by one line. This leads us to anticipate a rhyme for вышинé in the line after that, to complete a quatrain of alternating rhyme; but expectation is again thwarted, as this rhyme, too, is postponed for an extra line. The repeated process of delayed expectation lends particular dramatic weight and finality to the closing line of paragraph and part.

270-1 отягощённы...утомлённы: the spelling is archaic: in modern Russian, the short form of the past passive participle is invariably spelt with a single -н-.

285-96 Евгéний смóтрит...бéрега: several commentators have regarded Evgenii's boat journey as a symbolic crossing, the still fiery Neva (ll. 280-1) standing for the Styx (or in some variants the Acheron), the infernal river across which Charon, the ferryman of Greek mythology, transports the souls of the dead to Hades. Pushkin, as A.D.P. Briggs explains, seems to have depicted:

> an absurdly unreal occurrence in the midst of events taken from cruel actuality. A boat suddenly appeared out of nowhere...and [Evgenii] was transported across by a ferryman who charged him a *grivennik* (ten kopecks, only a small sum)... At that time

it is most unlikely that Evgenii would have met any ferryman still plying his trade, let alone doing it with good cheer, and one who would 'willingly' take grave risks for a derisory fee... This figure is beyond doubt a reminder of Charon, even down to the low-value [coin] which his clients had to pay.

(Briggs, 1991, p. 131)

It might be added that Charon had more than once figured explicitly in Pushkin's early poetry, and recurs in the work of K.D. Batiushkov and other contemporaries.

The journey of the living hero into the Kingdom of the Dead (cf. the bodies with which the 'other shore' is strewn in ll. 304-6) and his encounter with the shade(s) of the dear departed is a familiar component of classical narrative, but unlike Orpheus, Odysseus, or Aeneas, the lowly Evgenii makes no contact with his lost Parasha, and his journey is apparently one of no return. The symbolic underworld (or 'outerworld'!) into which he crosses (a pagan departure from the pagan city, at this point in the poem?) is perhaps essentially one of primal chaos: a state of solitude and disorder attendant upon exclusion from the ordered community, encompassing madness, rebellion, fear and eventual death.

296-9 Несчáстный...ужáсный: несчáстный – placed in prominent relief by the mid-line break (following the enjambement between ll. 295-6 which brings the preceding journey to an emphatic close), and rhymed with the already familiar and soon further recurrent ужáсный – succinctly encapsulates Evgenii's transformed essence. The enclosed rhyme of бежúт-глядúт is similarly evocative. Глядéть of course points backward, ultimately to Peter at the opening; but Evgenii, by contrast to the statuesque emperor, is henceforth a rootless wanderer in almost perpetual motion. Бежáть and бродúть become leitmotifs of his presence.

300-6 Всё перед ним...валя́ются: Pushkin uses an accumulation of passive constructions – past passive participles and reflexive verbs – to convey a scene of destruction which, whatever its symbolic connotations, is rooted once more in documentary evidence: both Aller and Berkh recorded the destruction on the outer reaches of Vasil'evskii Island, where the water had risen by sixteen feet and, according to Berkh, 'the majority of houses were damaged, many of them (инье) washed away to their foundations, every fence dashed down and the streets blocked with timber, wood and even [displaced] huts'. The gruesome detail of corpses strewn upon the streets is absent from official publications, but occurs in private eyewitness accounts such as that of S.M. Saltykova, soon to become the wife of Pushkin's close friend A.A. Del'vig.

314-19 Что ж э́то?...Где же дом?: since Evgenii's initial failures of recognition might seem to reflect the responses of a troubled mind increasingly divorced from reality, it should be noted that the basis of his experience remains authentic. Saltykova, whose impressions were probably known to Pushkin, told for instance of a sailor named Lukovkin, on duty during the day of the flood and so unable to return to his wife and three children in their home by the Gulf. When he was finally free to do so, 'he found neither wife, nor children, nor home, nor the slightest trace of his abode' (Izmailov, ed., p. 122). Many flood victims evidently perished along with their homes, and comparable stories of individual loss place in context Evgenii's apparent failure to verify his assumption that Parasha died in this way.

324 Захохота́л: typically, Pushkin conveys inner turmoil not by detailed psychological analysis, but primarily through description of external action. The laughter, evidently a sign of madness, might possibly be taken as implicit commentary on the reaction to the Russian capital by Mickiewicz's hero Konrad in 'St Petersburg', the third poem of *The Digression*: 'Pale-lipped with hate,/He laughed, raised his clenched fist, and struck the stone,/As though he summoned down a vengeful fate' (trans. Lednicki, p. 119).

328 У́тра луч: the morning ray glinting from behind 'tired' clouds might conceivably be taken as a symbolic return to the realm of light and order – for all except Evgenii, who is све́ту чужд (ll. 362-3; свет perhaps in the meaning of 'light' and 'world', as well as 'society' ?), and remains a creature of the gloom (мрак) in which he and the story have been plunged since the first line of Part 1.

332 багряни́цей: derived from багря́ный (*poet.; mod.* багро́вый, crimson, purple); used to denote the ceremonial purple mantle of the tsars, and figuratively (metonymically) to stand for the imperial power which the mantle represents. In context, the word seems to connote both Alexander's authority, and specifically the measures taken by him to alleviate the consequences of the flood; it may also evoke the conventional poeticism багря́ная заря́, thus implicitly equating the tsar with the light of 'rosy dawn'.

The element of irony in the implication that all 'traces' of evil misfortune have vanished (just as, perhaps, there is 'no trace' of a rhyme for следо́в in l. 331!) is developed throughout this paragraph.

335 свобо́дным: the primary meaning here is 'unencumbered', 'free of debris'; but the word doubtless retains strong (and ironic?) secondary implications of political – and moral – freedom.

336 С свои́м бесчу́вствием...вы́местить: Pushkin's depiction of 'people' (seemingly oblivious of their former divine terror), 'civil servants' and 'tradesmen' should perhaps be interpreted not only with reference to the predicament of the absent, seemingly forgotten Evgenii – a чино́вник now without прию́т, who *fails* to turn up на слу́жбу, and one *truly* robbed (огра́блен) by the thieving Neva, of all including his reason – but in contrast also to the official sententiousness of Berkh, who wrote that 'the first rays of the sun, illuminating a sorry picture of destruction, were witness to charity and compassion'.

343-4 С дворóв...лóдки: many boats and even large ships had been washed onto the streets by the flood.

344 Граф Хвостóв: Count Dmitrii Ivanovich Khvostov (1756-1835), a senator and prolific writer of bad verse, already the target of several epigrams and a parodic ode by Pushkin. Here Pushkin had in mind Khvostov's lengthy 'Epistle to N.N. On the Flooding of Petropolis, which Occurred on 7 November 1824' ('Послáние к N.N. О наводнéнии Петрóполя, бы́вшем 1824 гóда 7 ноября́'). The critic V.G. Belinskii's view that this reference to the incompetent Khvostov was an ill-judged piece of flippancy, out of keeping with the 'tragic fabric' of Pushkin's poem, has been echoed by many others; but it could reasonably be argued that it is in fact consistent both with the preceding catalogue of inadequate, inappropriate and unseemly responses to the flood (Khvostov was another who glibly underplayed its consequences, and stressed the ease with which normal order was successfully restored), and with an element of black humour which is a more sustained component of *The Bronze Horseman* than is generally supposed. The incongruous combination of петь – and even стихи́ – with несчáстье (and cf. несчáстный in l. 296) also points to the serious 'meta-literary' problem of the propriety or otherwise of *any* purely literary response to others' misfortune. Pushkin's multi-layered complexity is implicitly advanced as a compelling solution.

353-8 дум...пóлон...пусты́нный: further precise lexical repetitions again invite comparison and contrast with the description of Peter in the opening lines; пóлон is a more ordinary, less elevated form of the short adjective than полн in l. 2. Note, too, the re-introduction of the theme of dream, as also of the passage of time, implying a contrast between Evgenii's small, increasingly undifferentiated time scale, and the grand, precise historical sweep of l. 21.

360 бéдному поэ́ту: the possible identity of this 'poor' poet (the adjective suggesting a commonality with Evgenii even as his place is usurped) has prompted considerable conjecture. One school of thought detects an allusion to the Decembrist V.G. Kiukhel'beker (1797-1846), still held in solitary confinement in 1833; perhaps more attractive is the view that this is a tongue-in-cheek self-portrait, reflecting on the financial predicament with which Pushkin (a former inhabitant of Kolomna) was much preoccupied at this time.

364-70 пита́лся...стега́ли: the mixture of charity and aggression displayed toward Evgenii by the city's lowlier inhabitants apparently precludes any simple sociological conclusions. It should nevertheless be noted both that злы́е, the adjective previously used of the natural force of the waves, is transferred to the children, whose weapons of attack – stones – perfectly symbolise the now hostile essence of 'Peter's city'; and that civic hostility to those such as Evgenii had been enshrined in Petrine law: under Peter, beggars were theoretically banned from the streets of the capital and a fine of 5 roubles was imposed on those caught giving them alms. The adjective used to describe Evgenii's clothes echoes the description of Parasha's hut at the end of Part 1, and perhaps serves to invoke the thematic complex of 'opposition' of old to new.

377 Ни то ни сё: 'neither one thing nor another': the demonstrative pronoun сё, 'that', occurs only in a few such set expressions. It is perhaps further oblique evidence of Pushkin's surprising biographical empathy with Evgenii's predicament that a few months earlier, in February 1833, he had used the same phrase to describe his own circumstances in a letter to his friend P.V. Nashchokin: 'My life in Petersburg is neither this nor that (ни то ни сё), I have no leisure time, no free bachelor life...'. (The implicit attitude to 'bachelor life', however, is typically at odds with that quoted above in reference to l. 64.)

379-80 Дни...к осени: the date of Evgenii's second encounter with the statue is of obvious significance to the symbolic connection with the Decembrist Revolt of 1825 discerned here by many civic-minded commentators. But whereas ll. 386-7 closely echo earlier descriptions of the gloom and rain of cold 'November', reference to the declining days of summer in ll. 379-80 seems to place the encounter at a greater remove from 14 December: in a north-Russian context, probably in late August or early September. And although ll. 356-79 abound in temporal vocabulary (even to the etymological connotations of часовой – the state time-keeper?) the temporal uncertainty attendant upon Evgenii's apparent slippage from historical into seasonal-cyclical time (or even a temporal 'nowhere': cf. никогда in l. 372?) is compounded by the maximal vagueness of the adverb раз: strictly, there is no confirmation that this *is* the year immediately following the flood (i.e. 1825) and not one or more years later.

If Evgenii's moment of rebellion on Senate Square cannot fail to invite comparison (and contrast) with the Decembrists' actions, such obfuscation evidently attenuates any exact correspondence: 'Decembrism' may be one facet of possible meaning, but precise allegory was surely not Pushkin's intention.

384 челобитчик: the word derives from челом бить, 'to beat one's brow' (on the ground), i.e. to bow low, 'to kowtow', in petition. This is redolent of the non-Westernised, oriental customs of pre-Petrine Muscovy – apparently evoked once more in juxtaposition to the alien Petrine order of which the 'unhearing judges' can be regarded as a manifestation: Peter had decreed that judges in chancelleries should hear 'all manner' of petitions which had previously been addressed to the tsar himself. The simile describes waves less violent than during the autumn of the flood; the associated motif of resentment at lack of justice, which now implicitly aligns them with Evgenii, might equally suggest lengthy continuation of submissive discontent or the latent menace of a more forceful outburst to come.

401 ограждённою: alongside the surrounding passage's striking lexical parallelisms to the end of Part 1, the participle introduces a less obtrusive echo of the 'patterned railings' of the Introduction (l. 47). It is entirely typical of the poem's poetics that this second occurrence of the image of enclosure, in a much altered, negative context, should inevitably entail at least partial reassessment of the seemingly positive polemical value of the first.

403 Сидéл: this shift of posture (or perspective) has naturally given rise to much critical speculation concerning Pushkin's apparent diminution of Peter's stature. The Soviet commentator Iurii Borev has noted that it involves an element of realism, reflecting 'the laws of perception of [this] rounded sculpture, which "reads" differently from different angles'. From different vantage points around the statue, 'the Bronze Horseman appears to be either standing or sitting on his horse, either racing forward or rearing upward, rooted to the spot' (Borev, Iu., *Iskusstvo interpretatsii i otsenki: Opyt prochteniia* Mednogo vsadnika [Moscow, 1981], pp. 163, 165).

409 Тогó: the capitalised demonstrative pronoun recalls the capitalised personal pronoun in ll. 2 and 11: following the repetition of кумúр (l. 402), the implicit identification with a pagan demiurge is especially strong. By again withholding Peter's name, Pushkin is readily able to alternate his (or Evgenii's) focus between statue (e.g. ll. 410-11, 414-19) and human tsar (e.g. l. 412, 420), and perhaps to confound the two in the paragraph's concluding image.

413 Под мóрем: although под + place name can mean 'close to' (e.g. жить под Москвóй), the combination with мóрем is so strikingly unusual that the primary meaning of 'under', 'beneath', remains strong. An imputation of blame for the flood as the inevitable consequence of Peter's wilfully 'unnatural' act is thus combined with an intensification in this paragraph (cf. the rhyme возвышáлся/основáлся) of the 'vertical' imagery, the contrast of above (statue, tsar) and below (Evgenii, the basements and low lying, flood-prone areas of the poor) sustained throughout the poem.

421 над...бéздной: бéздна was used by Pushkin to mean both 'abyss' (with attendant connnotations of the chaotic void?) and (figuratively) 'sea'. Doubtless both meanings are intended here.

424 (424-42) Кругóм...обошёл...лик держáвца...тихóнько обра-щáлось: Borev has charted in detail Evgenii's path around the statue from the square behind:

> The bronze head of Peter is turned majestically and energetically rightward... If we follow Evgenii clockwise around the monument and look upward from a point in front and to the left, Peter's 'dread face' (грóзный лик) presents itself to us. An

observer continuing 'around the pedestal of the idol' will then gain
precisely the impression [recorded] by Pushkin: Показáлось...,
что... Лицó тихóнько обращáлось. If the observer moves
slightly further round and, 'pressing against the railings', that
is, from below and in front, looks up at the statue, a terrifying
picture confronts him: the enormous and powerful Bronze
Horseman, the hooves of his mount rearing over the observer's
head, will seem to hurtle irresistibly upon him, threatening to
trample and flatten everything that chances...into his path.

(Borev, p. 164)

From precisely this angle of approach, Evgenii's terrified flight supposedly
becomes entirely comprehensible.

426 взóры...навёл: cf. ll. 235-6. As Evgenii at last moves to face the
statue, the verbal echo serves to underscore the altered focus of this second
encounter.

428-9 Челó/К решётке: the railing which surrounded the statue in
Pushkin's day was more than shoulder-high although Evgenii, looking
upward at the image of the tsar through potentially symbolic iron bars, might
have been symbolically stooped (or kneeling). The use of the poeticism
челó recalls the челобитчик (and hence, for better or for worse, Evgenii's
pre-Petrine lineage) waiting before judges who accord no hearing (ll. 384-5),
and may thus serve as a prelude to revolt as well as a token of submission.
But челó also echoes the description of the statue in l. 415, just as the
adverb тихóнько, used of Evgenii in l. 394, subsequently refers to the
statute in l. 442. The constant undercurrent of comparison as well as
contrast between ruler and subject renders assessment of Evgenii's stature
at this point immensely complex.

436 чудотвóрный: Jakobson (p. 35) explains that 'the epithet
"miracle-working"...acquires a purely Pushkinian ambiguity in the madman's mouth: "creating miracles" as concerns Tsar Peter, and at the same
time "having originated miraculously", as concerns his statue'. The
potential blasphemy is clear.

438 Ужó тебé!: as a colloquial adverb, ужó means 'later,' 'later on';
combined with the dative it is a low colloquial expression of menace, with
the general meaning of 'just [you] wait'. Nicholas I reputedly objected to
Evgenii's outburst on the grounds that 'many would find it improper' for
Pushkin to allow a passer-by to threaten the figure of Peter the Great – 'and
for what, for founding [the city] on a spot prone to flooding'. But the
Symbolist poet Valerii Briusov observed:

Pushkin provides no more detailed elaboration of Evgenii's
threat. We never know precisely what the madman intends by his
Ужó тебé! Does it mean that the 'little' and 'insignificant' will
'later' prove able to avenge their enslavement, their humiliation

by the 'hero'?...There is no answer, and by the very vagueness of his expressions, Pushkin seems to be saying that the exact meaning of the reproach is unimportant. What matters is that the 'little' and 'insignificant' [man]...should suddenly have felt himself the equal of the Bronze Horseman, should have found within himself the strength and courage to threaten 'the potentate of half the world'.   (Briusov, pp. 46-7)

The solemn tone and abundant slavonicisms (чело́, хла́дной, пла́мень, обуя́нный, чудотво́рный) of the preceding sentences, which, as Briusov remarked, have no counterpart in earlier descriptions of Evgenii, might seem thoroughly consistent with the perception of a momentous inner transformation. But it could equally be argued that, after the lengthy rhetorical build-up of ll. 424-35 (perhaps, indeed, of ll. 404-35), the virtual – and increasing – incoherence of Evgenii's indeterminate, whispered threat, tailing off into the inarticulate silence of suspension points, instead constitutes the poem's supreme moment of (tragi-comic?) bathos. In that case, Evgenii's sudden malice is a product not of the clarity of rational thought suggested in ll. 404-5, but of the чёрная си́ла of insanity, into the grasp of which he now irredeemably relapses.

452 во всю ночь: the preposition would be redundant in modern Russian, where duration of action ('time during which') is expressed by straight accusative of unit of time + imperfective verb. The same meaning may also be expressed by в тече́ние + unit of time in the genitive.

453 Куда́...ни: 'wherever'. The addition of бы would be required in modern Russian, in which concessive clauses (introduced by 'whoever', 'whatever', 'whenever', etc.) are formed by the appropriate pronoun (кто, что, когда́, etc.) + бы + ни + past tense verb.

455 (444-55) и слы́шит...По...мостово́й...скака́л: in Pushkin's day, only the central streets of the capital were paved (with wooden blocks). Thus the 'thunderous' pursuit is located in the official heart of 'Peter's creation', not in the dirt- (or mud-) covered streets of the poorer residential districts. The lines which describe it are widely regarded as one of the most expressive instances of alliterative sound patterning in Russian poetry. Briusov saw the formal basis of Pushkin's onomatopoeic rendition of the 'heavy, resonating gallop' in the repetition of 'the same rhyming syllables' and 'the initial sounds of neighbouring words'; and in the particularly 'persistent reiteration' of the supporting consonants *g* and *k* (though *t* and *s* are no less prominent). Other formal features are handled to no lesser expressive effect. Hence, for example, the comments of one modern critic on the graphic distribution of rhyme:

As can be seen, Evgenij finds himself (stylistically) in the clutches of the Bronze Horseman: безу́мец бе́дный is sandwiched, as it were, between [the two occurrences of] Вса́дник

Ме́дный, [by whom he is] about to be destroyed. The significance of the passage is heightened by the use of lower case letters to depict Evgenij and capital letters to represent Peter; their stature vis-à-vis each other is thus confirmed.

(D. Burton, 'The Theme of Peter as Verbal Echo in *Mednyj Vsadnik*', *Slavic and East European Journal*, 26 [1982], p. 23)

456 с той поры́: 'from that time on'. The plural (с тех пор) would be required in modern Russian.

462 Карту́з изно́шенный: this is a civilian peaked cap – specifically not an attribute of the civil servant's uniform and the associated Petrine world of service Evgenii has now abandoned. His own hat was swept away during the flood (l. 234; perhaps a parodic allusion to the madness of Mickiewicz's Oleszkiewicz, who stands hatless to pronounce his long, rhetorical soliloquy against the tsar). The worn-out cap is presumably a charitable gift or cast-off.

464-5 О́стров ма́лый/На взмо́рье: this has frequently been identified as о́стров Голода́й (subsequently renamed о́стров Декабри́стов), rumoured to have been the unmarked burial place of the five hanged Decembrists. The geographical evidence is remarkably flimsy, however; for Golodai was inhabited, large enough for a mixture of factories and allotments, and hence, by Pushkin's time, an unlikely destination for Sunday (or 'Holiday', the name's possible etymology) outings. Other commentators have claimed to discern instead one of a group of much smaller neighbouring islands which have since merged into о́стров Декабри́стов; but more persuasive may be the view of Russian scholars such as V.F. Shubin, who writes that a 'vague recollection' of the burial place of the disgraced Decembrists may form an intentional part of the epilogue's emotional background, without having crucial significance. Shubin rightly emphasises instead the many detailed correspondences between the poem's beginning and end, and adds that the 'small island':

gloomy and empty, with the fishermen cooking their meagre supper, seems to be a corner of the earth which Petrine civilisation has passed by. It seems to bear no relationship to the ю́ный град [of ll. 21-2],...which has become alien and inimical toward Evgenii. The hero...finds his final resting place not in Peter's city,...but on an outcrop of 'pre-Petrine' land, the о́стров ма́лый, the image of which was suggested to Pushkin by any number of small islands in the Neva delta.

(V.F. Shubin, 'K topografii poemy *Mednyi vsadnik*', *Vremennik pushkinskoi komissii*, 22 [1988], pp. 146-9)

469-70 Или чино́вник...в воскресе́нье: Briggs points out that воскресе́нье not only suggests the holy day, 'reminding us of church-going', but also 'carries with it still some vestige of its original meaning, "Resurrection"' (воскресéние). A 'Christian or semi-Christian touch' is thereby introduced into the ending (Briggs, 1991, p. 132). At the same time, however, the *chinovnik*'s easy, unwitting attainment of Evgenii's unfulfilled dream – even his distantly implicit usurpation of Evgenii's projected role – entails an irony more readily apparent from Pushkin's drafts, where the description of Evgenii's thoughts had contained the lines: По воскресéньям лéтом в пóле/С Парáшей бýду я гуля́ть.

472-4 Наводнéнье...игрáя...Домúшко вéтхий: the combination of diminutive and adjective closely mirrors Evgenii's thoughts in l. 245 (вéтхий also looks back to the 'pre-Petrine' with which the word was first associated in l. 29). The inference that this is therefore Parasha's hut is generally accepted without question. Like Parasha's presumed death, however, Pushkin's text does not explicitly confirm the assumption it invites; and the curious introduction of the verb игрáть should give pause for thought. In conjunction with the implicit irony of Evgenii's resting place, the gerund might recall the notion of a cruelly mocking fate – the насмéшка нéба first evoked in the passage immediately following Evgenii's earlier thoughts of the вéтхий дóмик. But here the subject is not нéбо (with all that it might connote) but purely denotative, inanimate наводнéние; and it is not inconceivable that 'play' expresses not some cruel *design* of fate, but a pure randomness – in other words, this could be *any* 'dilapidated hut', a chance remnant of the flood which only a 'poor madman'(!) mistakes at his death precisely for that of his lost beloved. In the absence (or obliteration: cf. пуст/И весь разрýшен) of clear evidence, we should at least remain wary of too readily accepting the final grand coincidence of Evgenii's near- or posthumous- reunification with Parasha.

Connected with this is the 'ultimate question' of whether the universe is purposefully ordered – by Fate or God – or bereft of such order, fundamentally 'wild' (дúкий), 'abandoned' (пусты́нный), chaotic. The notes of cathartic restitution and religious reconciliation, seemingly uppermost in this final paragraph, are consistent with the notion of order; but once again, it seems, Pushkin maintains the possibility of a secondary reading, disruptive of overt meaning, which would incline toward the opposing alternative. In this latter case, of course, the imposition of meaning and order is a product of human will. It may prove illusory – like, in this version, the final delusion of the madman that he has recognised Parasha's hut – or triumphantly enduring, like Peter's (and the poet's?) creation of structure and history out of the primal chaos of which the imagery of the concluding paragraph reminds us. On this level too, the end of the poem points firmly back to the beginning, with a final striking contrast between its two main figures.

475-7 как чёрный куст...Свезлú на бáрке: it was not unusual for wooden peasant huts, generally made of whole logs laid horizontally upon one another and fastened at the end with wooden pegs, to be transported on wheels, by cart, or where appropriate, by water. Many huts were washed up entire by the flood; the comparison of this one to a 'black bush' recalls the primitive blackness of the huts in l. 7, reiterates the leitmotif of 'wood', and possibly retains implications of some 'underworld' kingdom of the dead.

478 У порóга: Briggs comments:

> the inference is not merely that Nature (or Peter or Fate) has demolished Yevgeniy, but that she (or he or it) has first been cruel enough to allow him tantalisingly near to the realisation of his modest ambitions, to the very threshold of a new life, before destroying him. (Briggs, 1991, p. 132)

481 рáди Бóга: the phrase means 'out of charity', 'for free'; but the literal implication of reconciliation with (or restitution of Evgenii to) a Christian God is evidently strong.

Bayley notes:

> In the final lines of the poem the brief sentences interrupt the rhythm, placing a full stop in the centre of almost every line; after the sonorous onomatopoeia of the charging horseman the effect is almost like Shakespearean prose following on the rhetoric of verse. Not only is the rhythm prosaic, it dies away into the mutter of the last line, with its feminine ending.
> (Bayley, pp. 163-4)

Pushkin's Notes

1 Альгарóтти...en Europe: Count Francesco Algarotti (1712-64), Italian Enlightenment author, described his stay in Russia during 1738-9 in *Lettere sulla Russia,* translated into French as *Lettres sur la Russie.* There is debate as to whether Pushkin took his vaguely attributed quotation direct from Algarotti, or at second hand. Of greater interest, however, is his refraction of the French source through the conscience of Peter in ll. 15-16 of the poem. Instead of the passive contemplation of the French verb *regarder*, the 'active' прорубить appears. This particularly suggests the use of an axe, and evokes the well-known practical image of Peter as enthusiastic carpenter-builder. The Russian verb also suggests rough force rather than sophisticated precision, however; and there is potential irony in the connection of the window which will bring Western light to Russian darkness not with refined Western tools, but with the traditional implement of the Russian peasant. Inevitably, too, thoughts of the axe might evoke the dark underside of Peter's wilful project of enlightenment. In Peter's own hands, the axe had also been a notorious instrument of execution.

2 стихи кн[язя] Вяземского: the immediate reference is to the third stanza of a poem by Pushkin's friend and literary associate, Prince Petr

Andreevich Viazemskii (1792-1878), entitled 'Conversation of 7 April 1832' ('Разговóр 7 апрéля 1832 гóда'):

Я Петербýрг люблю́, с егó красóю стрóйной,
С блестя́щим пóясом роскóшных островóв,
С прозрáчной нóчью – дня сопéрницей беззнóйной –
И с свéжей зéленью млады́х егó садóв.

[I love Petersburg, with its shapely beauty,
With its dazzling belt of luxuriant islands,
With its transparent night – unsultry rival of the day –
And the fresh verdure of its young gardens.]

The poem was dedicated to Countess E.M. Zavadovskaia (1807-74), and published a few months before Pushkin began work on *The Bronze Horseman*. Significantly, however, Viazemskii's expression of love for St Petersburg was formulated there in apologetic repudiation of his 'mad' (безýмный) invective *against* the city in the 'conversation' with Zavadovskaia to which his title refers. Pushkin would therefore have been mindful too of an 1828 poem by Viazemskii, which had opened with a striking statement of the contrary attitude: 'Я Петербýрга не люблю́'. This then unpublished (and unpublishable) piece, known only to a small circle of friends, was a vitriolic diatribe against the tense, inimical life of the imperial city, bureaucratically regimented under the eye of the Chief of Police. Pushkin had a manuscript copy in his papers, made for him by the author.

The footnote is thus one of several hints at the possibility of a diametrically opposed, negative perception of St Petersburg, present beneath, or in conjunction with, the overtly unclouded panegyric of the opening. The note seems significant, too, for its very unreliability. At first sight, it is flippant and inconsequential (given the abundance of literary sources on which the Introduction draws, why annotate only the relatively inconspicuous description of the White nights?; moreover, the resemblance of Pushkin's lines to Viazemskii's – once located – is in any case remote). This impression is partially offset by the more substantial underlying issue of conflicting attitudes to St Petersburg. But Pushkin's footnote proves misleading in another sense. Though his Introduction indeed owes a debt to Viazemskii, it is less to the poem indicated, 'Conversation of 7 April 1832', than to a piece entitled 'Petersburg: 1818' ('Петербýрг. 1818 гóда'). This contains a lengthy panegyric on 'Peter's city' (град Петрóв), raised from the marshes as a triumph of reason over the elements. Among other relevant details, it praises the city's military aspect; and Peter is said to live on in the 'eloquent bronze' (медь) of the Falconet statue, his protective, powerful arm a symbol of his readiness to turn to flight (бег/бежáть) and dispel the crazed malice (безýмная злóба; cf. Evgenii in ll. 436 ff.?) of Russia's enemies.

Such evocation of meaning through a process of misdirection is most pronounced in Pushkin's footnotes, but arguably models his procedures in the poem as a whole.

3 Мицке́вич...по́льского поэ́та: 'Oleszkiewicz', the concluding poem of Mickiewicz's *Digression*, was also entitled 'The Day Preceding the Inundation of St Petersburg in 1824' ('Dzien przed powodzią Peterzburską, 1824'). Its central figure, the Polish painter and mystic Oleszkiewicz, is shown mysteriously measuring the depths of the waters at dusk. He then makes two lengthy prophetic utterances aloud to himself. The first describes the impending flood as a Biblical disaster, the second of three great trials to be visited by Jehovah on Russia; his second utterance relates its coming to the misdeeds of Alexander I, who had sunk 'ever deeper under Satan's guile'. He had flouted the will of the Lord, and his nation would suffer accordingly.

'Oleszkiewicz' makes only passing mention of the winter weather and ice on the Neva; but Pushkin takes issue with this detail both as a significant recurrent element in Mickiewicz's symbolism of Russian autocratic oppression, here, 'in reality', impossible to justify; and more specifically, in refutation of the entire essence of Mickiewicz's apocalyptic message. If the very background to the scene Mickiewicz describes is manifestly inaccurate, then perhaps all that remain are 'beautiful lines' and 'bright colours', devoid of underlying substance. Pushkin's prosaic tale, it is implied, offers a 'truer' account.

4 Граф Милора́дович и генера́л-адъюта́нт Бенкендо́рф: Mikhail Andreevich Miloradovich (1771-1825), after a distinguished military career, was in 1818 appointed military Governor-General of St Petersburg; Aleksandr Khristoforovich Benkendorf (1783-1844) was head of the Corps of Gendarmes and the notorious Third (i.e. Secret Police) Department of the Imperial Chancellery. By 1833 he was in effect Pushkin's personal censor and direct intermediary in dealings with the tsar.

The exploits of both men in sailing forth to save flood victims were reported in some detail by contemporaries; and in one respect Pushkin's note could be held to give due acknowledgement of their heroism. The combination of text and authorial note nevertheless conveys an element of bathos, characteristic of this entire section of the poem, again employed to satirical effect. The four lines beginning Царь мо́лвил build to a crescendo at его́ пусти́лись генера́лы, the subject delayed by a string of prepositional clauses: but Pushkin's footnote (to which, unlike the lesser figure of Count Khvostov in Part 2, the names of the illustrious generals have been relegated) lists a mere two individuals: their 'launch' into official action seems ludicrously insufficient. This impression is apparently confirmed both by reference to Pushkin's drafts, which included a comic anecdote in which Miloradovich appeared in his boat at the window of Senator Count V.V. Tolstoi, and, once more, by linguistic register: the deflationary inclusion of colloquialisms (из концá в конéц, пустúлись) alongside such poetic turns of phrase as средь plus plural of водá.

Any settling of scores with Miloradovich (who had interviewed Pushkin before his southern exile in 1820) and Benkendorf also had a potentially darker implication, however. Both were actively involved in the suppression of the Decembrist Revolt; and Miloradovich was mortally wounded in the process, shot on Senate Square by the Decembrist officer Kakhovskii.

5 Смотрú описáние...из Рубáна...сам Мицкéвич: the first sentence refers to lines from Mickiewicz's description of the statue in 'The Monument of Peter the Great' ('Pomnik Piotra Wielkiego'), which read as follows in Lednicki's rhymed translation:

> His charger's reins Tsar Peter has released;
> It has been flying down the road, perchance,
> And here the precipice checks its advance.
> With hoofs aloft now stands the maddened beast,
> Champing its bit unchecked, with slackened rein:
> You guess that it will fall and be destroyed.
>
> (Lednicki, p. 122)

On the face of it, the lines provide a context which seems to resolve the apparent ambiguity of Pushkin's image: unlike in Mickiewicz, Pushkin's tsar exercises an iron control over his bridle; the contrast confirms that he is a figure of majestic vigour, who has raised his mount (= Russia) up, but will not plunge with it into the abyss.

Vasilii Grigor'evich Ruban (1742-95), however, was a mediocre 'loyalist' poet, historian and publicist, who had extolled above the wonders of the ancient world the 'true rock' on which Peter's monument was to be erected at the behest of Catherine the Great. Somewhat perversely, Pushkin therefore implies that Mickiewicz's 'oppositional' image of a chaotic imperial regime confronting inevitable downfall is derivative of Ruban's sycophantically conservative verses. This is an aesthetically and politically mischievous misreading, imputing to Mickiewicz (who had acknowledged Ruban with reference to one line only, not, as Pushkin implies, his whole poem) an inconsistency which, in his unswerving polemical purpose, he did not possess. A possible explanation is that – as occasionally elsewhere – Pushkin's comments on other writers in fact reveal rather more about himself: here, a perhaps agonised preoccupation with his own inconsistencies, his ability not so much to occupy a compromise position between two ideological extremes, as simultaneously to embrace both polarities. Once again, at the submerged level of his obscure footnote, Pushkin ultimately reinforces, rather than removes, the ambiguity of his own description in ll. 415-23.

NOTE ON VOCABULARY, STYLE AND TEXT

Vocabulary

The vocabulary includes all words found in Pushkin's text, with the following exceptions: words listed in *A First Russian Vocabulary* by Patrick Waddington (Bristol Classical Press, 1992); proper names; one or two examples of idiosyncratic usage dealt with in the Notes; the archaic-poetic forms of some common prepositions (вкруг, меж, пред, средь, чрез for modern вокру́г, ме́жду, пе́ред, среди́, че́рез); and the colloquial contractions уж, чтоб, of standard уже́, что́бы. In a handful of instances, a word which appears in *A First Russian Vocabulary* is used by Pushkin in a sense not given there (e.g. бить, обрати́ть, служи́ть, снять). Such words are included in the vocabulary with a translation appropriate to their context.

The vocabulary is limited only to the meanings in which words are used in the poem. However, the complexity of Pushkin's text has some-times made it desirable to suggest a wider range of near-synonyms or possible variant meanings than would be appropriate in the case of narrative prose. Not all variant translations will seem equally pertinent to all readers, and it will certainly be possible to discover additional nuances not indicated below. The vocabulary is no substitute for careful consulta-tion of reliable dictionaries.

Verbs are listed only in the aspect in which they occur. Past passive participles are given in the long form, and except where the verb has become obsolete in the modern language (e.g. подъя́ть/подъя́тый), are listed *under the infinitive from which they are derived*. Adjectives of participial origin (e.g. оживлённый) are listed in their own right, without reference to verbal derivation.

Where Pushkin uses obsolete or archaic variants of forms standard in modern Russian, the modern form is generally also supplied. Other morphological details, such as irregularities of declension or conjugation, are given only where relevant to Pushkin's specific usage.

The following abbreviations are used in the vocabulary:

adj.	(used as) adjective	*n.*	neuter noun
advb.	adverb	*obs.*	obsolete or archaic
coll.	colloquial	*p.*	perfective
dat.	dative	*p.a.p.*	past active participle
dim.	diminutive	*pej.*	pejorative
f.	feminine noun	*p.t.*	past tense
fig.	figurative(ly)	*pl.*	plural
ger.	gerund	*poet.*	poetic(ism)
hist.	historical term	*ppp.*	past passive participle
i.	imperfective	*prep.*	prepositional
instr.	Instrumental	*pres. part.*	present active participle
m.	masculine noun	*s.*	slavonicism
mod.	(in) modern	*sg.*	singular
	standard Russian		

'Slavonicism' indicates words taken from Old Church Slavonic. These often have a 'vocalised' Russian doublet (e.g. OCS бла́то, град: Russian боло́то, го́род, etc.), and tend to impart a solemn, archaic-poetic flavour to the narrative.

Obsolete stylistic features

Readers should be aware of the following recurrent syntactic and morphological features, not dealt with separately in the Notes or Vocabulary, in which Pushkin's usage diverges from the modern literary norm:

i) use of the short adjective in attributive positions (e.g. ве́шни дни, со́нны о́чи), where modern Russian invariably demands the long form.

ii) formation of some perfective gerunds to the same pattern as the imperfective, i.e. from the third person plural of the present/future tense: thus, e.g., уда́ря, утомя́сь, where modern Russian requires уда́рив, утоми́вшись.

iii) preference for neuter nouns ending in -ье. All such nouns in the text of the poem, with the exception of воскресе́нье (l. 470), end in -ие in modern Russian. In the vocabulary they are listed only as they appear in the poem.

iv) feminine instrumental singular endings in -ею, -ою, instead of -ей, -ой.

v) reflexive endings in vocalised -ся after vowels (e.g. оде́лася, where modern Russian has оде́лась).

i) would have been regarded as emphatically characteristic of an elevated poetic style; ii), however, was reasonably widespread in the prose as well as poetry of Pushkin's day, and would have been no more stylistically marked than other forms of the gerund (inherently, of course, a feature of literary rather than colloquial Russian). iii), iv) and v), were principally restricted to poetry, but only dimly perceived as markers of elevated style. iii) and iv) in particular long remained unexceptional features of Russian verse – essentially 'variant forms', usually selected according to metrical rather than stylistic considerations.

History and source of text

In December 1833 Pushkin chose to submit a manuscript copy of *The Bronze Horseman* to Nicholas I for his personal approval – possibly hoping that the tsar would prove less exacting than the official censorship, which had recently come under the control of the notorious ideologue S.S. Uvarov. The poem was returned with a number of deletions and question marks: against each occurrence of кумир and истукан, as well as against ll. 39-42, 410-14, 423 and 436-51. Unwilling to make the alterations necessary for his poem to appear in print, in 1834 Pushkin published only the Introduction – without the last five lines, and with rows of dots in place of the comparison between Moscow and St Petersburg in ll. 39-42. Two years later he reconsidered but soon abandoned the idea of reworking the entire poem in conformity with Nicholas's objections, making some adjustments of style and sense in the process. When he was killed in 1837, it therefore fell to his literary executor, the poet V.A. Zhukovskii (1783-1852), to prepare the first edition of *The Bronze Horseman* – in a version acceptable to Nicholas, which entailed some slight rewriting by Zhukovskii himself. The poem consequently reached its early readers without Evgenii's threat or the scene of his pursuit by the statue. Major and minor distortions were gradually and inconsistently corrected over the course of many years, but the combination of continuing censorship and competing authorial manuscripts made the establishment of a definitive text an extremely slow process. Even the prestigious Academy of Sciences edition of Pushkin's *Complete Works* (17 volumes; Moscow-Leningrad, 1937-59) did not completely resolve matters. A more thoroughly reliable text, prepared by N.V. Izmailov in the light of many years' archival study, eventually appeared in the 'Literaturnye pamiatniki' series only in the late 1970s (see Bibliography).

Izmailov's unstressed edition forms the basis for the present stressed text, in which, however, the words Бог and Божий have been capitalised, in conformity with Pushkin's rather than Soviet standard practice.

Marking of stress

In Pushkin's day a few participial forms may have had alternative pronunciations in е/ё (e.g. утомлённы/-ённы, смущённый/-ённый): in these cases the more modern, less ostentatiously archaic stressing in ё has been adopted. In accordance with the usual conventions in dealing with Russian versification, conjunctions and prepositions of two syllables and more have been considered unstressed (and thus, incidentally, there is nothing metrically untoward in Pushkin's use of и́ли in ll. 79, 81, 247; пе́ред in ll. 39 and 41; etc.). Exceptionally, despite the slight inconsistency, it has nevertheless seemed helpful to mark the stress on one or two such words where word stress and metrical stress coincide with a relatively strong logical stress (e.g. хотя́, l. 113; круго́м, l. 424).

VOCABULARY

А

адмиралтейский (*adj.*)
    (pertaining to) the Admiralty

Б

багряни́ца purple mantle
бал ball
ба́рка (wooden) barge
бег speeding, careering, gliding
бедня́к pauper, poor person
бе́дствие disaster
бе́здна abyss
беззабо́тный carefree,
    unconcerned
безлу́нный moonless
безмо́лвный silent, speechless
безу́мец madman
береговой (*adj. from* бе́рег) of
    the bank(s), shore
беспоко́йный restless
бессме́ртный immortal
бесчу́вствие insensitivity, lack
    of feeling
би́тва battle
бить (*i.*) to break, smash
би́ться (*i.*) to beat against
бла́то (*s.; mod.* боло́то) marsh,
    bog, swamp
блеск shine, brightness;
    brilliance, splendour
блесну́ть (*p.*) to gleam
бли́жний (*adj.*) nearby; (*noun*)
    neighbour (fellow being)
близёхонько (*coll.*) very near
блиста́ть (*i.*) to shine
боевой (*adj.*) battle

Бо́же God (*vocative*)
Бо́жий God's
бой (pre*p.* в бою́) battle, fight
бока́л (wine-) glass
боя́знь fear
брань (*f.*) swearing, abuse
бревно́ (*pl.* брёвны; *mod.*
    брёвна) log
брег (*s.; mod.* бе́рег) shore
броди́ть (*i.*) to wander
бро́нзовый (made of) bronze
бры́зги spray
бу́йный violent, wild,
    uncontrollable
бу́йство wild, unruly behaviour
бунтова́ть (*i.*) to rebel
бурли́вый turbulent
были́нка blade of grass
бьясь *ger. of* би́ться

В

ва́жный significant, substantial
вал (high) wave, breaker
валя́ться (*i.*) to lie around, be
    strewn
вглубь into the depths
вдали́ in the distance
вдаль in(to) the distance
вдова́ widow
верхо́м astride, on horseback
ве́тхий old, worn out,
    dilapidated
ве́чный eternal
ве́шний (*poet.*) vernal
вздохну́ть (*p.*) to (give a) sigh
вздро́гнуть (*p.*) to shudder

вздува́ться (*i.*) to swell (up)
взлома́ть (*p.*) to break up
взмо́рье sea-shore
взор gaze, glance
взрасти́ (*p.; p.t.* взрос, взросла́) to grow, spring up
властели́н (*poet.*) lord, potentate, master
влачи́ть (*i.; poet.*) to drag out (existence)
влива́ться (*i.*) to pour into
вне́млющий *pres. part. of* внима́ть (*obs. poet.*) to heed
вну́тренний inner, internal
возвыша́ться (*i.*) to tower above
возвы́шенный high, elevated
возгоре́ть (*p.; poet.*) to flare up
возмути́ть (*p. ppp.* возмущённый) to stir up, cloud; (*fig.*) to stir, incite to revolt
возмуще́нье indignation; turbulence; (*obs.*) revolt, rebellion
возмущённый (*adj.*) indignant; see also возмути́ть
вознести́сь (*p.; poet.*) rise up
во́инственный martial, warlike
вой howl, howling
волне́нье agitation
во́ля will
вопль (*m.*) wail, wailing
ворва́ться (*p.*) to burst, tear in(to)
вороти́ться (*p., coll.*) to return
воро́ты (*pl. only: mod.* воро́та) gate(s)
воспита́ние upbringing
воспомина́нье memory, recollection
во́я *ger. of* выть
вражда́ enmity

вса́дник horseman
всего́ in all (only)
всеча́сно (*obs.*) at any moment
вскипе́ть (*p.*) to boil up
вскочи́ть (*p.*) to leap up
вслед (+ *dat.*) after, in the wake of
всплыть (*p.*) to float up, surface
втечь (*p.*) to flow into
вчера́шний yesterday's
вы́местить (*p.*) to take sth. out on someone; to shift, pass onto
выть (*i.*) to howl
вышина́ heights, elevated position (в вышине́ aloft)

Г

генера́л general
ги́бнуть (*i.*) to perish
глава́ (*s.; mod.* голова́) head
гла́дкий smooth
глубина́ depth, depths
гнев (high) anger, ire
гне́вный angry
го́вор sound (of voices)
гордели́вый proud, haughty
грабёж robbery
гра́бить (*i.*) to rob, pillage
град (*s.; mod.* го́род) city
грани́т granite
граф count
графи́ня countess
гребе́ц oarsman
гри́венник (*coll.*) a small silver coin (ten-copeck piece)
гроб (*pl.* гроба́; *mod.* гробы́) coffin; (*fig.*) grave
грози́ть (*i.* + *dat.*) to threaten
гро́зный dread, terrible
грома́да huge mass, massive structure
грохота́нье crashing, rumbling
грудь (*f.*) breast

Д

даровáть, дарýю, -ýешь (*i.*) to confer, present

девúчий, -ья, -ье, -ьи girlish, maidenly

держáвец (*poet.*) sovereign, (supreme) monarch

держáвный powerful, sovereign

дéрзкий impudent; (*poet.*) audacious

дúво wonder, marvel

дичúться (*i.*) to avoid

добрó goods, property; (*coll.*) right!, right, then!

добы́ча booty, spoils

дóмик, домúшко (*m.*), *dims. of* дом

достúчь (*p.; p.t.* достúг) to reach

дрýжный well-acquainted, friendly

дýма (*poet.*) thought

дурь (*f.*) wild, headstrong behaviour

дыбы́ hind legs

дышáть (*i.*) to breathe

Е

едвá barely, scarcely, only just

едвá ли...не almost, practically; (be) on the point of

Ж

жáдный greedy

жúво vividly

жúвость (*f.*) liveliness, animation

З

забóр fence

забóта concern, anxiety

завалúть (*p.; ppp.* завáленный) to throw, strew into heap(s); to cause encumbrance thereby

завывáть (*i.*) to howl mournfully

задрожáть (*p.*) to (begin to) tremble, to give a shudder

задýмчивый thoughtful, pensive

заúмствовать (*i. and p.; ppp.* заúмствованный) to borrow

залúв gulf

заложúть (*p. ppp.* заложённый; *mod.* залóженный) to lay down (foundation)

замирáть (*i.*) (*fig.*) to run cold; to seize up

занестú (*p.*) to cast up

запáсливый provident, well-stocked

запечáтать (*p.; ppp.* запечáтанный) to seal

запировáть (*p.*) to (begin to) feast

запоздáлый late, belated

заря́ dawn, daybreak; sunset

затопля́ть (*i.*) to flood, submerge

захохотáть (*p.*) to break into loud laughter

звóнкий ringing, resonant

звучáть (*i.*) to sound

злúться (*i.*) to be ill-tempered, angry; (*poet.*) to rage

зло evil, harm, malice, spite; на зло (+ *dat.*) to spite

злóба anger, malice

злóбный malicious, angry, full of malice

злодéй (evil) villain

знáтный (*obs.*) well-born; member of the aristocracy

зреть (*obs.*) to behold
зы́блемый rippling

И
и́ва willow
игла́ needle
изве́стие, изве́стье (piece of) news, account, information
изнемога́ть (*i.*) to grow weak from exhaustion
изно́шенный worn out, threadbare
изобража́ться (*i.*) to be portrayed, depicted
ино́й other(s)
и́стина truth
истука́н (*obs.*) idol, statue

К
казнь (*f.*) punishment, execution
кана́л canal
ка́пать (*i.*) to drip, fall (in drops)
карту́з cap
ки́нуться (*p.*) to fling oneself
кипе́ть (*i.*) to boil
кладби́ще (*mod.* кла́дбище) cemetery
клокота́ть, -очу́, -о́чешь (*i.*) to seethe, boil up, gurgle
клони́ться (*i.*) to move towards, pass into
клуби́ться (*i.*) to swirl, billow
ко́е-ка́к somehow or other
конь (*poet.*) horse, steed
копы́то hoof
корма́ stern
котёл, -ла́ cauldron
краса́ (*obs.*) beauty, ornament
краси́вость (*f.*) beauty
красова́ться (*i.*) to stand out in beauty

кресто́м in the form of a cross; сложи́ть кресто́м to cross, fold (arms, etc.)
кров shelter
кро́вля roof
круши́ть (*i; coll.*) to ruin, wreck
куми́р (*poet.*) idol (*esp.* statue of pagan divinity)
кусо́к piece
ку́ча cluster, huddled group
кучерско́й coachman's

Л
лампа́да icon lamp; (*obs.*) lamp
ла́па paw
лени́вец lazy-bones, idler
лик (*obs. poet.*) face, visage
ликова́ть (*i.; poet.*) to exult, rejoice
ло́вля fishing
ломи́ть (*i.; coll.*) to break (up), smash
лоску́т (*pl.* лоску́тья) tattered piece of material, tatters
лото́к, -ка́ (street-trader's) stall
луч ray
любова́ться, -у́юсь, -у́ешься (*i. + instr.*) to admire
любопы́тный curious
люд (*coll.*) (group, class of) people

М
ма́лый small
мгла mist, darkness
мгнове́нно instantly, immediately
ме́дный copper; (*poet.*) bronze
месте́чко (*coll.*) job
мета́ться (*i.*) to toss (and turn)
мину́вший past, preceding

молва́ (*obs.*) rumour, news, gossip

мо́лвить (*p.; obs. poet.*) to say, speak

мостова́я roadway (cobbled part of street)

мочь, не в unable, in no condition to

мо́щный mighty

мрак (*poet.*) darkness, gloom

мра́мор, мра́морный marble

мра́чный gloomy

му́ка torment, pain, suffering

муче́нье (state of) torment

мши́стый mossy

мяте́жный mutinous, rebellious

Н

навести́, -еду́, -еде́шь (*p.*) to direct (at)

наводне́нье flood

на́глый brazen, insolent

надме́нный haughty

наймы́ = отда́ть в наймы́ (*mod.* внаймы́) to rent out

наси́лье violence, force

насквозь (all the way) through, clean through

насме́шка mockery, ridicule

настава́ть, настаю́, -аёшь (*i.*) to begin, dawn

насы́титься (*p.*) to have one's fill, sate oneself

нахо́дка find, (*coll.*) godsend

небреже́нье (*obs. poet.*) unconcern, lack of attention

неве́домый (*poet.*) unknown

не́вод (large) fishing net, sweep net

недально́й (*coll.*) limited, dull-witted

недви́жный (*obs. poet.*) still, immobile

незави́симость (*f.*) independence

неколеби́мый (*poet.*) unshakeable, firm

некра́шенный unpainted

нена́стный bad, foul (of weather)

неподви́жный immobile

нере́дко frequently

нести́сь (*i.*) to rush

нищета́ poverty, destitution

носи́ться (*i.*) to be borne, swept along

ны́не nowadays

О

обло́мки (*pl.*) debris, wreckage

обойти́ (*p.*) to go round

обрати́ть (*p.; ppp.* обращённый) to turn

обраща́ться (*i.*) to turn

обру́шиться (*p.*) to collapse, cave in

обуя́ть (*p.; ppps.* обуя́лый, обуя́нный; *obs. poet.*) to seize, grip; render helpless

оглуши́ть (*p.; ppp.* оглушённый) to deafen, stun

огра́бить (*p.; ppp.* огра́бленный) to rob, pillage

огра́да fence, railing

огради́ть (*p.; ppp.* ограждённый) to fence off, around

одино́кий solitary, lonely

однообра́зный uniform; monotonous

одоле́ть (*p.*) to overcome

оживлённый animated, lively

озари́ть (*p.; ppp.* озарённый) to light up, illumine

околдова́ть (*p.; ppp.* околдо́ванный) to cast a spell over, bewitch

око́шко *dim. of* окно́

окре́стный surrounding

омрачи́ть (*p.; ppp.* омрачённый) to darken, plunge into gloom

опусте́ть (*p.*) to become empty

о́пытный experienced

оса́да siege

осе́нний autumn, autumnal

основа́ть (*p.; ppp.* осно́ванный) to found

основа́ться (*p.*) to be founded

остервени́ться (*p.*) to be filled with frenzy, wild rage

отва́жный courageous

отсе́ль (*obs. poet.*) hence, from here

отча́янный desperate; despairing

отяготи́ть (*p.; ppp.* отягощённый) to weigh down

о́чи (*obs. poet.*) eyes

очути́ться (*p.*) to find oneself, (come to) be (somewhere)

П

па́сынок stepchild; (*fig.*) foundling, outcast

пелена́ (*poet.*) cover(ing); shroud

пе́на foam

пе́нистый frothing, foaming

пе́ня (*obs.*) complaint, lament, reproach

перево́зчик ferryman

перегради́ть (*p.; mod.* перегороди́ть; *ppp.* перегражде́нный) to block up, obstruct

перекли́ка́ться (*i.*) to exchange shouts, cries with; call to

Петро́в, Петро́вый (*obs.; possessive adjs.*) Peter's

пехо́тный infantry

пиру́шка (*dim. of* пир, feast) get-together; dinner; binge

пита́ться (*i.*) to eat, live on

пла́мень (*s.; m.; mod. n.* пла́мя) flame

плен captivity

плеска́ть (*i.*) to splash

плеть (*f.*) whip

пловéц, -ца́ (*obs.*) mariner, voyager

победи́ть (*p.; ppp.* побеждённый) to conquer, vanquish

побе́дный victory, victorious

побежа́ть (*p.*) to break into a run, rapid motion

повествова́нье (*poet.*) story, tale, narrative

по́весть (*f.*) tale, story

пови́снуть (*p.; p.t.* пови́с) to hang

повле́чься (*p.; obs. poet.*) to set off, wend one's way

повсю́ду everywhere, all over

пого́ня pursuit

погрузи́ть (*p.; ppp.* погружённый) to immerse, submerge

пода́ть (*p.; ppp.* по́данный) to give (in charity)

подва́л cellar

подёрнуться (*p.*) to be covered over, misted

подмыва́ть (*i.*) to wash (from beneath)
подно́жие pedestal
подо́шва sole
подро́бность (*f.*) detail
подыма́ть(ся) (*i.; coll.;* = поднима́ть(ся)) to raise, lift up (to be raised, lifted up)
подъя́тый (*obs. poet.*) (up)raised
пожи́тки (*no sg.; coll.*) belongings
покида́ть/поки́нуть (*ppp.* поки́нутый) to leave, abandon
поко́йный the late, deceased
покры́ться (*p.*) to be covered
полно́щный (*obs. poet.*) midnight; (*fig.*) northern
полуми́р half (the) world
поме́ркнуть (*p.; p.t.* поме́рк) to grow dim; (*fig.*) to fade
поро́г threshold
порфироно́сный (*poet.*) purple-clad, imperial (i.e. wearing imperial robe)
поспе́шный (too) hurried, hasty
поте́шный (*obs.*) (intended for) amusement, military exercise or spectacle
пото́п flood (*also Biblical*)
потрясе́ние shock
потрясти́ (*p.; ppp.* потрясённый) to shake
поу́тру (*mod.* поутру́; *coll.*) (early) in the morning
похорони́ть (*p.*) to bury
почи́ющий (*obs. poet. fig.*) slumbering, resting (in the grave)
по́яс belt; по по́яс up to the waist
пра́вить (*i. + instr.*) to rule

пра́здный idle, with no occupation
преда́нье legend, tradition
предме́стье settlement near a town or city; suburb
предше́ствовать (*i. + dat.*) to precede
пре́жний former, previous
препоручи́ть (*p.; obs.*) to entrust
приба́вить (*p.*) to add, increase
прибежа́ть (*p.; past. part.* прибежа́вший) to come running
прибыва́ть (*i.*) to rise, swell
прижима́ть (*i.*) to press, clasp to, against
при́зрак ghost, apparition
прикова́ть (*p.; ppp.* прико́ванный) to chain, shackle
прикры́ть (*p.; ppp.* прикры́тый) to cover (over, up); to assuage
приле́чь (*p.; p.t.* прилёг, -легла́; *coll.*) to press against
примеча́ть (*i.*) to notice
при́стань (*f.*) quayside, landing stage, pier
при́ступ assault
прича́лить (*p.*) to moor, put in
прию́т shelter; (*poet.*) sanctuary; abode
пробежа́ть (*p.*) to run through
прозва́нье (*obs.*) surname
прозвуча́ть (*p.*) to be heard, resound
прозра́чный transparent
происше́ствие occurrence, event
проруби́ть (*p.*) to cut, hack through
просну́ться (*p.*) to wake up

простере́ть (*p.; ppp.*
    простёртый; *ger.* простёр-
    ши) to stretch out
просто́р expanse, spaciousness;
    на просто́ре (*fig.*) at large;
    expansively, free of
    constraint
прострели́ть (*p.; ppp.*
    простре́ленный) to shoot
    through
проясни́ться (*p.*) to become
    clear
пунш punch
пусти́ться (*p.*) to begin (rapidly),
    launch into; to set off
пусты́нный uninhabited,
    deserted, desolate
пу́ще (*coll.*) more, more strongly
пы́шный luxuriant

Р

разбе́г run, running start;
    с разбе́га with momentum,
    at speed
разбира́ть (*i.*) to discern,
    distinguish, comprehend
разбо́йник robber, bandit
разлучи́ть (*p.; ppp.*
    разлучённый) to separate,
    part
размечта́ться (*p.*) to dream,
    become absorbed in reverie
размы́ть (*p.; ppp.* размы́тый) to
    wash, sweep away; to erode
размышле́ние thought,
    reflection
разруше́ние destruction
разру́шить (*p.; ppp.*
    разру́шенный) to destroy
разъяри́ть (*p.; ppp.*
    разъярённый) to infuriate,
    fill with fury

рать (*f.; poet.*) (military) host,
    (assembled) ranks
рва́ться (*i.*) to tear; to strain
    (attempt to break free)
реве́ть (*i.*) to bellow, roar
реде́ть (*i.*) to thin
решётка railing(s); grille;
    (prison) bars
родня́ (*collective sg.*) relatives,
    relations
ро́за rose
роково́й fateful
ропта́ть, ропщу́, ро́пщешь,
    ger. ро́пща (*i.*) to murmur,
    grumble (in discontent)
рыболо́в fisherman

С

сбира́ться (*i.; coll.; mod.*
    собира́ться) to intend
сбро́сить (*p.; ppp.*
    сбро́шенный) to throw,
    fling down
сбы́ть (*p.*) to subside, fall
свет light; society; world
свирепе́ть (*i.*) to rage
свире́пый savage, ferocious
свози́ть/свезти́, *p.t.* свёз,
    свезла́ to take (down, away),
    clear away
сдви́нуть (*p.; ppp.* сдви́нутый)
    to displace
сей, сия́, сие́, сии́ (*obs.; prep.
    sg.* сем) this
серде́чный heartfelt
сжать (*p.*) to clench; to squeeze,
    press, or fold tightly together
сия́нье shine
скака́нье galloping
скака́ть, скачу́, ска́чешь (*i.*) to
    gallop
скала́ cliff

скита́ться (*i.*) to roam, wander (protractedly)
ско́рбный grieving, sorrowful
скре́жет gnashing, grinding
скриви́ться (*p.; coll.*) to become crooked
скры́ться (*p.*) to disappear
след trace
сло́вно as if, like
служи́ть (*i.*) to work in civil/government service
слыха́ть (*i.; coll.*) to hear; to sense, notice
смени́ть (*p.*) to replace, succeed
смире́нный humble
смири́ться (*p.*) to become compliant, subdued
смиря́ть (*i.*) to temper, subdue
сму́тный (*poet.*) troubled
смущённый embarrassed; confused
смяте́нный (*obs. poet.*) troubled, perturbed
смяте́нье anxiety, inner turmoil
снести́ (*p.; ppp.* снесённый) to demolish; to sweep away
снять (*p.*) to remove, take away
совладе́ть (*p.*) to cope with, master; to co-rule
сойти́ (*p.*) to get off, come down
сокры́ть (*p.; mod.* скры́ть; *ppp.* сокры́тый) to hide, conceal
со́нный sleepy, somnolent
сорва́ть (*p.*) to tear off
соста́вить (*p.; ppp.* соста́вленный) to compose, compile
спра́виться (*p.*) to consult
спря́тать (*p.; ppp.* спря́танный) to hide, conceal
спя́щий *pres. part. of* спа́ть to sleep

срок (fixed) period of time, term
старина́ days, times of old
стега́ть (*i.*) to lash, whip
стесни́ться (*p.*) to tighten, become constricted
сти́снуть (*p.*) to clench
стихи́я element(s), elemental forces
сто́гна (*s.; obs. poet.*) wide street, square
столб column
стопа́ (*obs. poet.*) (foot)step
сторожево́й (*adj.*) sentinel, on guard, guardian
сторо́нкой (*advb.; coll.*) giving sth. a wide berth; keeping one's distance from sth.
страши́ться (*i.*) to fear
стремгла́в headlong
стреми́ться (*i.; obs.*) to speed, move swiftly
строй formation
стряхну́ть (*p.; coll.*) to take, shake off, throw (casually) aside
ступе́нь (*f.*) step
судья́ (*m.*) judge
суждённый destined, fated, preordained
су́мрак twilight
су́мрачный gloomy
счастли́вец fortunate person
сыма́ть (*i.; coll.; mod.* снима́ть) to take off

Т
тверды́ня (*obs. poet.*) stronghold, fortress
творе́нье creation
терза́ть (*i.*) to torment
тесни́ться (*i.*) to crowd, press closely together

тече́нье current, flow
тихо́нько (*coll.*) slowly, gradually; submissively
тлеть (*i.*) to smoulder; to rot, decompose
това́р goods, merchandise
тогда́шний of that time
толкова́ть, толку́ю, -у́ешь (*i.; coll.*) to talk, expatiate
толпи́ться (*i.*) to crowd, throng
тону́ть (*i.; pres. part.* то́нущий) to drown
то́пкий swampy
то́пот tramp, tread, clatter
топь (*f.*) wet, swampy ground
торга́ш (*coll.; pej.*) (small) tradesman
торжество́ triumph
торжествова́ть, торжеству́ю, -у́ешь (*i.*) to celebrate
торопли́вый hurried
тоска́ melancholy, anguish, depression
трево́га anxiety, alarm
трево́жить (*i.*) to trouble, disturb
тре́петный tremulous; frightened
труди́ться (*i.*) to toil
труп corpse
тужи́ть (*i.; coll.*) to grieve
тще́тный futile, vain
тьма (*poet.*) darkness

У
убо́гий wretched, benighted
убы́ток loss
увы́ alas
уголо́к (*dim.* of у́гол) corner; (small) part of a room, rented out
ужа́сный awful, terrible; dread, inspiring awe, terror

ужо́ (*low coll.*; used with dative of person to threaten vengeance, retribution)
узда́ bridle
узо́р pattern, tracery
умири́ться (*p.; obs. poet.*) to reach a peace with, become reconciled
унима́ться (*i.; coll.*) to abate
уныва́ть (*i.*) to lose heart, be dejected
уны́лый mournful, cheerless
успоко́ить (*p.*) to (offer, maintain in) calm; provide conditions for peaceful existence
устоя́ть (*p.*) (*fig.*) to stand firm
утоми́ть (*p.; ppp.* утомлённый) to tire, weary
утоми́ться (*p.*) to tire, become tired of

Ф
фи́нский Finnish

Х
хи́жина small hut; small, meagre dwelling
хи́щный predatory, rapacious
хлад, хла́дный (*s.; mod.* хо́лод, холо́дный) cold
хлеста́ть (*i.*) to lash
хлы́нуть (*p.*) to surge, gush forth
холосто́й (*adj.*) bachelor

Ц
цари́ца tsarina, wife of tsar
ца́рский tsar's, imperial

Ч
часово́й sentinel, sentry
чело́ (*obs. poet.*) brow

челобитчик (*hist.*) petitioner, supplicant

чернéть (*i.*) to be black

честь (*f.*) honour; respect

чёлн small boat, dug-out; (*obs. poet.*) (small) boat

чинóвник (*hist.*) civil servant (*esp.* lowly clerk), functionary

чинóвный (*adj. from* чинóвник)

чугýнный cast-iron

чудотвóрный miracle-working (*usu. of icons*)

чýждый (*adj.*) alien, (like a) stranger

чухóнец (*obs. pej.*) Finn

чýять (*i.*) to sense

Ш

шáйка gang, band

швед Swede

шепнýть (*p.*) to whisper

шинéль (*f.*) greatcoat (item of civil servant's uniform)

шипéнье hiss, fizzing

Over sixty Russian Texts are available or in production in this series, all with English introduction and notes. They include the following:

Pushkin: Boris Godunov, V. Terras
Pushkin: Eugene Onegin, A. Briggs & F. Sobotka
Pushkin: Little Tragedies, V. Terras
Pushkin: The Queen of Spades, J. Forsyth
Pushkin: Tales of the Late Ivan Petrovich Belkin, A. Briggs

In the Critical Studies series:
Pushkin's The Queen of Spades, N. Cornwell
Pushkin's The Bronze Horseman, A. Kahn
Pushkin's Eugene Onegin, S. Dalton-Brown

Text with Translation:
Pushkin: Selected Verse, J. Fennell

CPSIA information can be obtained at www.ICGtesting.com
Printed in the USA
LVOW04s1100240814

400662LV00015B/569/P